# PRAISE FOR THE AUTHOR

*I've been a franchisee in two different franchises since 2002. In the past few years, since knowing Sharon Jurd, I have seen her display commitment, dedication and passion for franchising in a range of areas. I am impressed with Sharon's application to her own franchise as well as her tireless work in training, mentoring and assisting others to develop and grow their own business through franchising.*

*Sharon is constantly moving ahead in developing strategies and ideas that can be implemented in any business to grow and achieve the desired goals. As a franchisor she is always available to assist, encourage and lead her franchisees as well as others interested in any franchising venture. Her success is undoubtedly due to her positive outlook as well as her commitment and desire to help others succeed.*

**Julius Czerney**
**International Author & Speaker**
**'Dead One Day, Laughing the Next'**
**Franchise Owner**

---

*I have had the pleasure of knowing and working with Sharon on a number of projects over the last ten years, both within and outside of the franchising industry. Sharon can best be described as positive energy. She actively seeks to work with others, to inspire and assist them to grow, not only to achieve their goals but also to reconsider what is possible and go beyond that.*

**Simone Pentis**
**Managing Director**
**Advantage Partners Lawyers**

---

*Strong, vibrant, positive and infectiously enthusiastic are but just some of the words that I would use to describe Sharon Jurd.*

*Having known Sharon for more than 6 years, I can say that I hold her in the highest regard, not just as a client but also as a friend and colleague in the franchise sector. Sharon is a woman of integrity, vision and passion demonstrated both in her business and personal life.*

*Sharon has been recognised and awarded the exclusive award of Australian Franchise Woman of the Year which is a major achievement in the franchising industry.*

*Having been involved in the Franchising industry for many years I admire Sharon's positive attitude to compliance and her measure of quality that requires near perfection.*

*Sharon is always giving of her time and wisdom to other franchisors and franchisees that is invaluable to their success and growth.*

*She is a mentor, motivator and innovator and is literally a breath of fresh air for the business sector and it is a pleasure to know and work with her in her businesses.*

**Derek Sutherland**
**Special Counsel**
**HWL Ebsworth Lawyers**

# EXTRAORDINARY WOMEN IN FRANCHISING

**Global Publishing Group**
Australia • New Zealand • Singapore • America • London

# EXTRAORDINARY WOMEN IN FRANCHISING

## How Their Businesses Have Grown And How Yours Can Too...

FRANCHISE WOMAN OF THE YEAR #1

BRAZILIAN BEAUTY

Foreword by
**Kym De Britt**
*General Manager*
*Franchise Council of Australia*

SHARON JURD

DISCLAIMER

All the information, techniques, skills and concepts contained within this publication are of the nature of general comment only and are not in any way recommended as individual advice. The intent is to offer a variety of information to provide a wider range of choices now and in the future, recognising that we all have widely diverse circumstances and viewpoints. Should any reader choose to make use of the information contained herein, this is their decision, and the contributors (and their companies), authors and publishers do not assume any responsibilities whatsoever under any condition or circumstances. It is recommended that the reader obtain their own independent advice.

First Edition 2015



National Library of Australia
Cataloguing-in-Publication entry:

Creator: Jurd, Sharon, author.

Extraordinary Women In Franchising : How Their Businesses Have Grown And How Yours Can Too / Sharon Jurd.

1st ed.
ISBN: 9781922118868 (paperback)

Franchises (Retail trade)
Women-owned business enterprises – Australia.
Businesswomen – Australia.
Entrepreneurship – Australia.
Small business – Australia.
Success in business – Australia.

Dewey Number: 658.87080994

Published by Global Publishing Group
PO Box 517 Mt Evelyn, Victoria 3796 Australia
Email info@GlobalPublishingGroup.com.au

For further information about orders:
Phone: +61 3 9739 4686 or Fax +61 3 8648 6871

*I dedicate this book to all of the women making a difference in other people's lives, sometimes without recognition or acknowledgement. You are the answer for someone.*

Sharon Jurd

# ACKNOWLEDGEMENTS

It has been a great privilege to be able to write this book. There are a number of people to whom I would like to say, 'Thank you.'

To all of the women in franchising who have taken a leap of faith and franchised their business to expand their product or service to help others and change other people's lives. Your dedication and non-stop commitment to your cause must continue, there are people out there who need you.

To all of the women in my life who have inspired me, challenged me, motivated me and just loved me, I thank you.

I would like to thank the Franchising Council of Australia for their support and encouragement throughout my franchising journey and with this book. A special thank you to Ralph Edwards, you were the first person I met from the FCA and you welcomed me and my business into the franchising community with open arms. I would like to thank Derek Sutherland, my franchising solicitor, because of you the legalities of franchising have been a breeze and I have complete trust in you to protect me, my business and my franchisees. Thank you to all of the members on the QLD/NT FCA committee for all of your support. I would also like to thank some amazing women in the franchising industry who have inspired me, supported me, encouraged me and shown me the way: Simone Pentis, Alicia Hill, Tamra Seaton and Kate Baring.

A HUGE thank you to the extraordinary women who are featured in this book. Your willingness to share your knowledge and experience will undoubtedly help other women to follow in your steps in both business and franchising. It has been a tremendous honour and privilege to work with you on this book and through your stories and insights many lives will be influenced for the better.

A special thank you to Darren Stephens, who is not only my publisher, but my mentor. You keep opening my eyes and heart to a bigger and better life. Without your support I could not have changed so many people's lives in such a short time and for that I'm truly grateful.

To Jackie and Helen and all of the team at Global Publishing, I love our chats, our laughs and our jokes. Thanks for not only making my book but also me look so good. You are truly amazing and professional people. Thank you to my distributor, Dennis Jones and Associates, for their support in the distribution of my books.

To my dad and mum, Kevin and Wendy George, you have always encouraged me to be the woman I have always wanted to be. I love that you are the biggest supporters in my life and in every business venture I have undertaken.

To my two children, Jacob and Casey Jurd, you have grown into amazing adults. I have never been more proud of you. I love you! xx

To my sisters, Sonya Moore and Kylie George, you are the most amazing women I know. So often you are my strength when I need it most. You are such wonderful mothers.

To my four nieces, Tegan and Darcie Moore and Daisy and Ruby Nugent, you make me proud every day. I know that as you grow you are fast becoming strong, independent and driven young women in your own lives and careers. Your mothers have guided you perfectly. I am so blessed to be a part of your life and look forward to being a part of all your future achievements.

And finally, to my life and business partner, John Sanders, our franchising journey has been amazing! We didn't listen to the negatives and kept forging ahead to that light at the end of the tunnel. You challenge me to be a better businesswoman every day and I like that! I love you! x

**EXTRA BONUSES!!**

To help you Grow Your Business Fast I have included a Bonus Offer of a further 7 top tips from myself and 6 other successful business people.

These tips will help you to reach your goals and give you important information crucial to people who are in business for themselves!

**Special Report**
**(Valued at $97.00)**

## "7 Top Secrets Revealed By Highly Successful People"

**To Access This FREE Report**
**Simply Go To**
**www.SharonJurdEvents.com.au**
**And Download It.**

# CONTENTS

# FOREWORD

On behalf of the Franchise Council of Australia, it is my pleasure to support this work by franchisor, educator, FCA committee member and Australian Franchise Woman of the Year, Sharon Jurd.

Australian franchising is rich in entrepreneurship, collaboration and community.

It is through this community ethos that the founders, CEOs and innovators of some of Australia's best-known franchise brands share their history and insights on the following pages.

Women have always played an important role within the Australian franchise community. The Franchise Council of Australia supports this through both the Women in Franchising Committee and the annual Franchise Woman of the Year award, some of the winners of which, appear in this book.

Australia has the honour of claiming best practice when it comes to franchising. We have some of the most robust regulations, some of the most consistent growth and among the highest concentration of franchised business units per capita in the world.

The Griffith University Franchising Australia Report 2014 notes that there are 1,160 active franchise systems in Australia, encompassing 79,000 individual franchisee businesses and employing more than 460,000 Australians. Resources like these, showcasing the founders of businesses that exemplify the Australian mentality of getting in there and having a go are so valuable to the Australian economy and are incredibly important.

This book is a rare chance to understand the way a simple idea can turn into a fledgling business and eventually transform into a household name. It is your opportunity to learn from people who believed in their ideas, took risks and created a business not only for themselves but a network of businesses that have enabled everyday Australians to achieve things they'd never have been able to, without these leaders in Franchising.

*Kym De Britt*
**General Manager**
**Franchise Council of Australia**

# INTRODUCTION

When someone asks me, "If you had your time over again, would you go into franchising?" I say a definite, YES! It has been an amazing experience for me. Has it been challenging? Yes. Has it been scary? Yes. Has there been a time when I thought, "What in the hell am I doing here?" Yes. But all of these have been fleeting moments in a positive environment.

The franchising industry is a power house industry and can bring rapid business growth. It enables business owners to expand and grow a brand from a small owner operated business to a large international company.

Is franchising for everyone? No. If you're not passionate about your product, service or system and are only looking to make a 'quick buck' then franchising is not for you. This is a dedicated industry and not for short term gain. If you want exponential growth of your business and increased sales of your product or service worldwide, then franchising may be an option for you.

When you franchise, you have the opportunity to change people's lives. It may be by giving your franchisee the opportunity to own their own business and earn the income and lifestyle they deserve or through the end consumer where your product or service has a profound impact on their lives. Either way, it is a gift that you can give to someone else.

If you are thinking about franchising, buying a franchise or looking to grow your franchise business, this book will help you if you take on these amazing lessons that I have shared with you and action them into your life and business.

In this book you will hear from some extraordinary women who have not held back and have told it like it is. These interviews are their own experiences and stories, there are no PA's or PR companies writing the correct answers. These women have answered the questions from their heart during an audio recorded interview with me and that's why this book is so profound and meaningful. Never before has a collective group of women got together to share their insights into the franchising industry in this format.

You will read about their successes, their challenges and even their sacrifices. What they had to do to sell their first franchise and how they took their brand and made it into a household name. They will share their secrets to their marketing and their management styles. These ladies will also let you know when the best time was for them to franchise. These top performers will share with you who inspires them and what keeps them motivated each day and week and you may even be surprised by their answers to these questions.

My first experience with franchising came in 1986 when I was employed in a small franchising group, even though franchising wasn't that popular in my area back then. Later on, I became involved in the largest real estate franchise in the world where I owned two franchises, before commencing franchising and becoming a franchisor. During my time in the franchising industry I have gained and shared a huge amount of knowledge and have had the pleasure of spending time with business owners at the top of their game. When I was awarded the Australian Franchise Woman of the Year award, I walked off stage where everyone was congratulating me, then something was said that resonated with me. It was suggested that I should look at the previous winners of this award and realise the significance and the exclusivity of winning it. They also mentioned that there are women not only in franchising but in business aspiring to achieve what I had just achieved. They also suggested for me to take some time to really appreciate the award.

I took this advice. I knew some previous winners but I took some time to really appreciate the other women who had previously won the award but during my research I found that there was really no place for women (or men) to go to find inspiration and motivation from other highly successful women in franchising. I found that these women were out doing so many amazing things but no one was sharing their strength, courage and determination for others to follow. This is what inspired me to write this book; now there is a place for aspiring franchisors and franchisees to go.

# CHAPTER 1

**SHARON JURD**
HydroKleen Australia

# CHAPTER 1

**SHARON JURD -**
HydroKleen Australia

*Work fast! Get so far in front of your competitor that they can't catch you.*

*Sharon Jurd*

After dominating the real estate industry Sharon Jurd took a new direction and became the director of HydroKleen Australia, growing the franchise system from scratch to the largest franchise in its industry and cementing it as the leader in its field.

Sharon is passionate about helping people grow businesses quickly using very simple strategies that give massive results. Sharon is very passionate about being consistent and persistent.

In only 4 short years HydroKleen Australia has become a national franchise with more than 30 franchisees. The company is now expanding internationally under the banner of HydroKleen Global. Sharon is the CEO of Sharon Jurd Events where she shares her knowledge of business growth with business owners through several mediums including: 12 Week Business Academy – an online business growth program, her Dreams to Reality 3 day signature event and one-on-one coaching programs.

Sharon's professional achievements have been recognised through winning over 36 industry and business awards such as Franchise Business of the Year, People's Choice Award, Chamber of Commerce Business of the Year, Gold Coast Business Excellence Award - Emerging Business, QLD/NT Franchise Woman of the Year and the Australian Franchise Woman of the Year, just to name a few.

Sharon's nature of giving back is highlighted by her contribution to and membership of the Franchise Council of Australia and Variety Children's Charity. She is also on the FCA Women in Franchising National Committee and the Franchising Council of Australia's Queensland Committee.

Sharon has a real passion and love for changing people's lives. It is heart-warming to her to be a part of someone's change for the better.

**Tell us a little about yourself and your company**

I grew up in a country town called Singleton which is in the Hunter Valley in New South Wales. I left high school at the end of year 10, at the age of 15. I had part time work in retail and at a local hairdressing salon while I was at school. I always thought I was going to be a hairdresser but it wasn't to be. I started full time work at a grocery store called

Franklins but I wasn't happy just being on the checkouts, I wanted to be in the cash office as I felt it could be a better job and it was prestigious. When the job became vacant I went to the manager and said, "This job's mine." He said, "I'm sorry Sharon, you have to be 18 to be in the cash office." Then I said, "I resign." I didn't, but I went looking for another job and found one in a real estate office soon after, called Col Simpson & Co. Little did I know that the office was part of a small franchise company. In 1986 in this country town, franchising wasn't that well known or understood but this commenced my almost 25 year career as a real estate agent, business agent, stock and station agent and auctioneer. In 2004 I opened my own real estate office in another small country town called Muswellbrook under the franchise company Century 21 and became market leader within 12 months. I opened my second office in my home town after the franchise became available there. It was just 12 months later, in 2005. After my successes in the industry I sold both my offices in 2009 and 2010. In 2010 I joined with my partner and started to develop our franchise company HydroKleen Australia in Darwin. 12 months later we moved our lives and the business to the Gold Coast, Queensland. I also own the franchise HydroKleen Gold Coast, international company HydroKleen Global and Sharon Jurd Events which is my business growth specialist company.

**Tell us about the company's current position. How are things tracking and what is the vision for the business?**

HydroKleen Australia is a national franchise and in 4 years has grown to more than 30 franchisees. We will reach 70 franchisees in total in the next 4 years which will be close to our maximum for Australia. This year we have placed a general manager in HydroKleen Australia to grow the Australian brand and our focus is to expand internationally with our company HydroKleen Global. Our growth is strong with many national and international enquiries which is very exciting.

"We knew our niche and we didn't stray from that."

**What do you think were some of the factors that contributed to your company's exciting growth?**

We knew our niche and we didn't stray from that. We service and clean air conditioners. We don't sell air conditioners and we don't install air conditioners. We are the specialists in what we do.

"We took everything that customers hated about tradies out of our business."

We moved fast because we knew that in 4-5 years we would have other companies trying to compete. We had to make cleaning your air conditioners exciting. We developed the systems, the processes and the equipment to give the customer an exceptional experience. We took everything that customers hated about tradies out of our business. We don't turn up late (or not at all). We don't leave a mess. We explain what we are doing and have great follow up systems. And we don't have the coveted bum crack!

**What are some of the most exciting changes you've experienced?**

When we first started in the industry no one knew who HydroKleen was or what we did. Over time, our brand awareness has grown to people changing their dialogue from, "We clean our air conditioners" to "We HydroKleen our air conditioners." It is pretty exciting when people are saying this. I can remember when I was at a networking function and I said what my business was and a lady said, "I know what that is!" I was thinking, "No, she doesn't" but then she said, "You HydroKleen air conditioners." I could have kissed her! I thought to myself, "I have made it! All the branding is paying off and someone finally knows what we do."

We implemented a new customer relationship management and booking system into the HydroKleen system and it was a massive jump into advanced technology for our franchisees but they were ready and they embraced it. It has dramatically reduced time output in all areas of the franchisees businesses allowing them to get on with what they are good at.

**What do you believe your biggest sacrifice was in getting the business off the ground?**

At the time I didn't think of sacrifices but looking back, there were things that changed. Money was the first thing. I came from owning my very profitable businesses to having no income. My partner is in the business as well so we didn't have any other source of income. We had to manage money very carefully.

Time was next. I thought that after selling my real estate offices I was going to work less – how wrong I was!

At first the business was the only focus and we didn't spend as much time with family and friends as we should have. In fact, I moved to the Gold Coast knowing only John's sister and her family and after 18 months I realised that I had not made any new friends in this area. So I had to really change that balance in my life.

> "I expected everyone to keep up with me"

**If there was one key area in management that you would do differently, what would it be?**

I expected everyone to keep up with me and now I realise that people will meet the goals on time but in their own way. I'm more flexible on 'how' they get there, as long as they get there.

**What would you say have been the highlights so far for your business?**

There are many! I always stop to celebrate all of the little successes along the way like setting our first office up, hiring a new team member, innovation of a new product, our first franchisee and conducting our first franchisee training.

Our franchisee conference every year is always a major highlight; catching up with all of our franchisees and celebrating the wonderful year we have had as a whole.

For me, firstly it was winning the FCA QLD/NT Franchise Woman of the Year and then going on to win FCA Australian Franchise Woman of the Year. That was just amazing for me, considering we had only been franchising for 4 years. Being appointed on the QLD/NT FCA Committee is still very exciting.

Becoming an author was a major achievement for me with my first book being published in November 2013. This was something that seemed so far out of reach before it became a reality.

> "Work fast! Get so far in front of your competitor that they can't catch you."

**What tips would you give to other businesswomen who are getting into business?**

Work fast! Get so far in front of your competitor that they can't catch you.

Remember your business is not about your product but about the customer's experience. Build the experience.

> "Know your ideal customer. "

Do not listen to negativity. Loads of people told us our goal of 12 franchisees in our first 12 months was ridiculous. We ignored them and we brought on 13 franchisees in 13 months. If we had listened to them we would have had 1 or 2 franchisees for the year. Were we naïve? Maybe, but we achieved what we set out to do.

"There is always more to learn."

Know your ideal customer. Get to know them very well and then communicate to them effectively.

**When did you first discover that you had entrepreneurial talent?**

It wasn't a defining moment but when I opened my first real estate office it was just easy. I made a lot of mistakes but for the most part, the right answers came easily. Some people would ask, "How do you know that?" I don't know, I just do. I just know what has to be done. I use a lot of common sense, intuition and logical thinking.

I have a real clarity of where I am heading and what things are going to look like in 5, 10 and 15 years.

"That's all we had to give; our time."

I know I am an entrepreneur but just not 'exactly' sure how I got here. I believe that learning from others, taking that knowledge on board and implementing it gave me the courage to do more. There is always more to learn.

**What is your approach to marketing and how did you get your name out into the marketplace?**

When we first started we didn't have any money for marketing let alone for budgeting. We did everything we could with as little as possible. Our first 6 franchises were referral based, as are most of our franchises, but after that, databasing was huge for us. Initially we identified air conditioning companies as our ideal franchisees so we contacted every air conditioning company in Australia and asked them if we could send them some interesting industry information. This was time consuming but that's all we had to give; our time. We couldn't afford national advertising campaigns. We contacted everyone, and I mean everyone, we knew and told them what we were doing and asked if they thought it might interest someone they knew. After air conditioning companies we went to electricians and other tradies in certain target market areas.

We used any free media we could get. If it was free and it was a positive story line, we were basically there.

We used networking, from a corporate level to a local level. We had to educate our consumer about cleaning and servicing their air conditioner as most people don't realise that they have to do it or that it is government legislated in the workplace.

**What are your top tips for effectively branding a business?**

Be strong! Keep the branding consistent and don't allow anyone to dilute your brand one little bit. We use the same font, we use the same graphics, we use the same uniforms, we use the same vehicles and most importantly we use the same message.

You have to be persistent. You can't start putting your message out there, then stop, then start again. Once you start don't stop.

Be clear and precise with your message. A confused consumer will not buy.

Know your ideal customer and then get your brand in front of them all of the time.

**When did you know that it was time to think about franchising the brand?**

We were very different from most brands. Before we had even named the business we were building it to franchise. From the start we built everything to scale up into a large franchise model. We were always making decisions based on national and international expansion. It's not natural for me to think small.

We piloted two franchises in Darwin to test and measure our systems, our marketing, our processes, our dialogues and equipment. After many changes we were happy to add other franchises to the brand. We actually waited until the 1st July 2010 to issue documents so we could include some legislation changes in them.

**How did you promote and sell your first few franchises?**

As I said in a previous question, the first 6 or so just heard about what we were doing and wanted to be a part of our business and came on board very quickly. Our referral strategies still sell more franchises than any other strategy. The next 6 or so were from referrals and our databasing.

"Even though we were new and small we were professional about what we did.

We encouraged our enquirers to call our franchisees and talk to them about our system, ask them about us and our support.

I believe our marketing material looked very professional and our training and support were ongoing so that was comforting to the person enquiring. Even though we were new and small we were professional about what we did.

**How did the brand evolve, from start-up till now, in how you market?**

We have always been targeted in our marketing; firstly to air conditioning companies. Then we went to particular local marketing areas because we wanted to be truly national and not dominating in just one state. We have now expanded to the franchising expo and recently attended the Sydney expo because we want to expand our coverage in Sydney.

Social media and the online world play a major part in our marketing strategy and every year this becomes more focused. We encourage our franchisees to participate socially as well.

We learnt how to better leverage free media and how PR can grow our franchisees businesses.

Our franchisees use no cost or low cost marketing strategies in their own local marketing area.

"We had to use every dollar wisely."

**What has been one of the biggest challenges you have had to face in the franchise business and how did you overcome it?**

Managing cash flow especially early on. We had to use every dollar wisely. It sharpened our skills in this area to a whole new level. I didn't realise you could do so much with so little cash.

Managing people. Every one of our franchisees are very different. Sure, they have the same passion for the brand, they have the drive for success and they love being a part of the HydroKleen family but what I learnt very quickly is that they are driven by very different factors; some money, some time and some lifestyle. Each relationship is different and has to be treated that way.

Finding and building relationships with long term suppliers. At first we were not being diligent enough in our choices. The suppliers would let us down and not deliver correctly so we took a good look at the supply chain and re-established relationships with companies that had similar high standards of customer experience as us.

"Communication is the key."

**What is the most important thing(s) you have learnt about successful franchising?**

Communication is the key. You must let every stakeholder know what is happening. We now have regular teleconferences, newsletters and our intranet system is regularly updated so the franchisees are up to date and can communicate freely with us.

When you start franchising, be willing to change very fast. We thought we had our model all figured out but within 12 months we knew we had to change. With a lot of discussion, advice, thought and research we acted on this very quickly and are ever so grateful we made the change.

**In your opinion, what are the most common mistakes new franchisors and franchisees make?**

Franchisors don't have good systems and procedures in place. They don't train correctly initially or continually. They don't communicate well. They don't have a good marketing strategy for their franchisees.

Franchisees sometimes think that the franchisor is going to run their business for them. They sometimes think the franchisor has all of the answers and will never make mistakes.

**What do you believe are the essential qualities and attributes of a successful franchisor or franchise system?**
A successful franchisor clarifies the expectations of the incoming franchisee from the beginning. They communicate what is expected from the franchisee and what is expected from the franchisor.

There is great training and support for the franchisees. They have a great communication system. They have great local marketing strategies.

The system must have happy, profitable franchisees.

> "The system must have happy, profitable franchisees."

**What advice would you give to someone who is thinking about investing in a franchise?**
Ask lots of questions. Ask the franchisor, ask the franchisees, ask supplier companies. Take advice from people who are in the know. Spend time getting all of the information to make an informed choice.

> "The opportunity presents at the right time"

Don't take notice of people who do not understand your dreams and goals – not everyone will get you and what you want to achieve. If you listen to them you will never make the choice to move forward.

**From your perspective, what stops people from being successful?**

Not thinking big enough! People miss the opportunities when they are presented to them. The opportunity presents at the right time so you have to take the action. You can't say, "I'll wait till next month or next year" as the same opportunity will not be there.

People wait until they know everything but they will never know everything.

**What do you believe are the essential qualities or personal attributes of a successful person?**

They are driven, they never ever give up. They have clarity about what they want to achieve. They can communicate their goals to other people and bring them along on the journey.

**What do you think holds people back from achieving their goals?**

Fear of what people might say. People will tell them that it can't be done or that they are not good enough and the embarrassment if the idea doesn't work.

"Do not have a plan B."

**How would you describe your management style?**

Fair, direct, fast! I love consultation and delegation. People know exactly what I am aiming to achieve. I expect people to do what they say they are going to do, in the time frame in which they said they would. No excuses!

**What are your secrets to being a successful businesswoman?**

Do not have a plan B. If you have a plan B it is easy to say, "I'll just fall back on that if this fails" and you will. Have your business set up as a no fail option.

If you want to achieve something, go get it! Don't wait for someone to bring it to you.

A successful businesswoman is determined; they are super organised. They are always prepared whether it be a board meeting, conference, stakeholder meeting or supplier meeting. They are never over emotional about decisions that have to be made.

**How do you stay focused and on track daily and in the long term, especially when times get tough?**

I work with an ideal day and week. I focus on my ideal day to be consistent and persistent in the business. I have allocated time for myself, health and wellbeing first. I like to know that at the end of the week all of the tasks are done.

I have my goals in front of me and around me all of the time so I can be reminded of why I am doing this and what I want to achieve.

"My team helps me with focus."

I have family, friends and mentors that help me say focused. Sometimes just calling your 'bestie' brings back your positive attitude.

My team helps me with focus. If I wander into the office without focus and they are all over it, it encourages me to pick up my game.

**Who would you say has inspired you in the past?**
Different people have inspired me in different ways at different times in my life. As my goals change so does the person who is inspiring me.

"If you are consistent and persistent you will succeed."

People who are out there changing people's lives. People who have overcome adversity. Those quiet achievers.

Darren Stephens from Melbourne inspired me to become an author. Karen Scott from New Zealand inspires me to not be scared.

My partner John inspires me to be a better person in life and in business.

**As a top successful businesswoman, what do you hope to inspire in others?**
That they can do it too. They don't have to be extremely talented or extremely knowledgeable or extremely wealthy. Whether you're female or male, whether you are white or black, whether you are educated or not – none of that matters. They already have it within them to succeed.

"You can achieve more than you think you can."

If you are consistent and persistent you will succeed.

**What does success mean to you and how does one achieve it (have more of it)?**
I measure success as little achievable steps in my journey. It's not something at the 'end' because I don't want to get to the 'end'. What was

successful to me 10 years ago is quite different now. Every time you do something for the first time should be measured as success because once you have experienced that feeling or learnt that skill it cannot be taken away from you.

To become successful you have to keep expanding your comfort zone, so what was once out of your comfort zone becomes your new normal.

To have great relationships with family and friends. Have the flexibility in my life to take a day off, jump on a plane or in the car and be where I need to be.

**What is the most important piece of advice anyone has ever given you?**
'You can achieve more than you think you can.' I thought about this for a very long time before I realised, "Yes I can!"

**What drives you to continue and grow even further?**
I love that I can help other people to become successful. I can change their life. The more I do the more I can help others. I might only play a small part but that small part to me is huge!

The unknown. I hate not knowing so I want to get there as fast as I can so I do know…for example: How big can this business grow?

"He who controls your time controls your money."

**Is there a significant quote or saying which you live your life by?**
'He who controls your time controls your money.' I truly believe this.

I don't want anyone else controlling (or limiting) my income. I stay in control of how I spend my time. I spend the majority of my time on income producing activities. If some people try to distract you in business, don't let them, they do not have the same goals and dreams as you.

**What are some of your future plans or goals (personal or business) for the next 5 – 10 years?**
For HydroKleen it is to be at saturation point throughout Australia. It's to establish ourselves internationally and to be known on the world stage.

For Sharon Jurd Events I want to continue to expand the brand, especially my 12 week Business Academy online program, globally.

For me personally, I want to experience all of the successes that come along with all of that.

**What is your greatest passion in life?**
Personally, I love to travel! I work hard and fast so I can travel. It gives me the greatest experiences that I can hold onto forever. When it comes to birthdays and Christmas and the like I ask my partner to buy me experiences, not things. Things can be taken away but experiences are truly yours, forever.

I love to influence change in others' lives.

I am passionate about growing businesses.

I love the quality time I get with my partner and family, it's priceless.

**How do you want to be remembered?**
As a nice person.

For someone to say, "Because of you I'm a better person and I have a better life."

*Keep the branding consistent. A confused customer will not buy.*

# CHAPTER 2

## JANINE ALLIS

Boost Juice

# CHAPTER 2

## JANINE ALLIS -
Boost Juice

*I think if you surround yourself with great people, great things will happen.*

Janine is an adventurer at heart, travelling the world as a young Aussie backpacker in the 80s, working as anything from a camp counsellor in San Francisco to a stewardess on David Bowie's yacht.

In 1999 during a trip to the US, Janine witnessed the juice and smoothie category growing steadily. Upon her return to Australia, Janine studied the local retail sector where she noticed a distinct lack of healthy fast food choices. After extensive research, she began to develop a business concept that was different from anything else in the world. Her vision was to "do retailing differently," delivering a unique customer experience based on the "love life" philosophy. In 2000, Boost was born.

Janine's leadership style is natural, warm, giving and extremely demanding, which has created a high performance culture in her business, achieving amazing results.

Janine has been presented with numerous retail, franchise and business awards including Telstra Business Woman of the Year, Amex Retailer of the year, Exporter of the year and this year BRW named her one of fifteen people that changed the way Australia does business in the last 35 years, just to name a few.

Janine and Jeff (Janine's husband) were looking at expanding upon the Australian Boost business. The strategy was to utilise the solid foundation that had been created with Boost to be able to bolt on new and exciting brands and enable them to maximise their growth potential. Salsas Fresh Mex Grill was the first and in 2007 they purchased a 4 store business which now has over 50 stores Australian wide. In December 2012, Retail Zoo acquired CIBO Espresso, the Italian espresso bar franchise that has wowed Adelaide for 12 years. CIBO Espresso shares the simple pleasures of the Italian lifestyle - wonderful coffee and quality food - in a stylish bar setting. It has 21 stores in Adelaide and three in Brisbane. Under the guidance of Retail Zoo, expansion is underway.

Their new baby in the business is a chicken shop call Hatch, which has huge potential in the Australian market.

There are almost 7,000 people working across the four businesses under the holding company Retail Zoo, for which Janine is now a director.

Retail Zoo has over 400 stores that have turned over just on $2 billion dollars since inception. Boost Juice bars are also in more than 12 countries outside of Australia.

Based in Melbourne, Janine is a working mother of four. Her life is hectic so she understands firsthand the demands the world can put on an individual! Janine is an advocate for a healthy lifestyle and maintains a five-day-a-week yoga practice and is a very average surfer and tennis player...but loves both.

**Quick facts:**

Janine is 49 years old and works alongside her husband, Jeff Allis. They have four children: Samuel (23), Oliver (17), Riley (16) and Tahlia (6) and live in Victoria.

Boost Juice started in 2000 from a kitchen table in the suburbs of Melbourne.

Janine started working at 17 and has tried her hand at multiple jobs. She started her career as a media assistant at the advertising agency, McCann-Erickson, and went on to modelling, working as an assistant manager in a gym, a nanny in France, a promotions executive in Portugal, a camp counsellor in the USA, a stewardess on David Bowie's yacht in the Mediterranean (now that was fun!), a senior manager for a cinema chain that launched in Singapore, a publicist for United International Pictures (rubbing shoulders with famous actors and directors), a publisher, an author, touring agent for USA comedians, then Boost Juice and now Retail Zoo. There are some interesting stories in that lot!

Achieved a 95% consumer awareness rating in the first 5 years.

Through the GFC, continued to grow the bottom line by over 20%.

Sales of over 250m pa.

Over 400 stores in 12 countries.

Acquired Salsas Fresh Mex Grill four years ago with 4 stores and now have over 50 stores.

Was a director of the Hawthorn Football Club for three years, which ended in 2009.

Is a director and minority shareholder of Kikki K, a top end stationery and giftware company.

Won Telstra Business Woman of the Year in 2004.

In 2013 was in the top 100 of most admired women in Australia.

Made the women's honours role in 2007.

For more information visit http://www.boostjuice.com.au/about

**Tell us a little about yourself and your company**

I was born in Australia. I grew up in the eastern suburbs of Melbourne with a fairly standard upbringing. I went to a tech school. I left school when I was about 16 years old and worked full-time until I was 21. I went on an adventure for the next 7 years, travelling around the world.

I came back to Australia then met and married my gorgeous husband. We then had a couple of children and I decided I didn't want to work for someone else any more. That was in 2000.

> "Make sure you're bigger this year than last year."

We started to formulate a plan with regards to a number of businesses. We had a couple businesses that failed and then Boost Juice Bars was born. We went from 0 to 100 stores in the first 4 years. In 2015, we have 3 brands over 400 stores in 15 countries.

**What's the vision for the company?**

The vision for our company is to continue to grow and innovate. Success for any business out there is to make sure you're bigger this year than last year. It's that constant battle of how to find growth and how to increase profit. It's that constant view of excellence and improvement.

**You've won a lot of awards along the way, for example, Telstra Business Woman of the Year and Franchise Woman of the Year. What was your reaction to being the recipient of those prestigious awards?**

What happens when you're working in a business is that you're so preoccupied by the next problem or the next deal that needs to be done or the next store to open that you tend to not stop and actually look at what you have achieved or how far you have come on the journey. Those awards are a great reflection on the journey to date.

> "Those awards are a great reflection on the journey to date."

I was so busy that I never really got to network with any other women or really network with anyone so it was an opportunity to stop, reflect and actually meet a bunch of dynamic, exciting women with whom I could continue to build relationships and share business experiences with in the future.

"Surround yourself with great people, great things will happen."

**What do you think were some of the factors that contributed to your company's exciting growth?**
I think that if you surround yourself with great people, great things will happen. I was very lucky to marry a man who I think is one of the most talented marketers and strategists in Australia.

It was just the logical way of looking at business. It was always considering the customers and what they wanted and driving as hard as we could to achieve those goals.

**What are some of the most exciting changes you've experienced in the business?**
I'm not sure if there have been changes necessarily but there's evolution. I think that there's never been a big revolution of Boost. It's always had the same vision of "love life" and just trying to make someone feel that little bit happier about their day and also helping people be healthier.

The evolution of the business is really understanding how the market moves. When we started, there was a little bit of email. There really wasn't any social media. TV was one of the main sources of people's entertainment. The press and radio were second and third.

You can now order online, you no longer need a piece of cardboard or five cards. You have it on your iPhone. How we communicate with our customer now is very different from how we used to and how we promote and reward and delight our customer is also different from how it used to be.

> "The biggest sacrifice for anyone starting a new business is time."

I think it's just being aware of where the trends are going with regards to social media and with regards to health and diet and making sure that we're on top of it and we're always looking to please our consumer for their feedback.

**What do you believe was your biggest sacrifice in getting the business off the ground?**

I think the biggest sacrifice for anyone starting a new business is time. You've only physically got so many hours in a day and you not only have work but in my case I had three children at the time and as well as a husband and I've got my own needs too so something has to give. You certainly tend to give up your own needs first.

Quite often, I felt like I was doing everything. Quite often, I was the parent who always took their child to school in the wrong uniform and took them to school when there wasn't school. I just physically did not have time to be great at everything.

> "You certainly tend to give up your own needs first."

It was just managing that time and finding systems and solutions to enable me to not have things fall through the cracks. So the day that I took my child . . . well, the days (there were a couple of times), to school without school being on, you get there and you go, "How come I can get a parking spot? I shouldn't be able to get a parking spot."

"It was like, "Okay, what can I do? How can I create a system so that it doesn't happen again?" You put a system in place and it may happen again but it'll happen less often.

> "You put a system in place and it may happen again but it'll happen less often."

**If there was one key area in management that you would do differently, what would it be?**
In the early days, it was putting up with the wrong people in the wrong roles for too long. We get so caught up in 'we've got so much to do' that when the person is adequate in that job we just leave them there and just overlook all the things that are going wrong because 'I'm just too busy to rehire and retrain.'

When you look back in hindsight, you go, "I should have moved quicker because then all of these disasters wouldn't have happened." I think you need to trust your intuition. Quite often, if you think something's wrong, normally, there is something wrong.

> "If you think something's wrong, normally, there is something wrong."

**What would you say has been the highlight for your business so far?**
The first time we hit 100 stores, the first time we hit $1 million, the first time we opened in the international market, the first time we sold some equity and took some money off the table and the first time we created a new brand to bring into the Retail Zoo.

"Hire great people"

I think the firsts are always quite exciting because when you do firsts, it means that you've had some strategy that you've put into place and then you've worked out how to make it a reality. Instead of still talking about it, you've actually made that happen.

**So what tips would you give to other businesswomen who are getting into business?**

The tips for a businesswoman or businessman tend to be quite similar 90% of the time. Hire great people, put great systems in place and make sure you know your numbers and that's not gender-specific.

I would say to women, particularly women with children, set yourself up to succeed before you go down the path of business or executive roles. Make sure you have great day care. Make sure you have great family support. Make sure you have a job that has that flexibility and where they trust you to be able to do the work at home if you need to.

I think it's important that if you set yourself up instead of trying to wing it, then it certainly helps with success rates. For me, I always had an office that was within 2 kilometres from my home and it was always within 2 kilometres from the school. I could always attend all the school functions. I was very lucky that my mum lived around the corner so she could support me with raising the children.

"Set yourself up to succeed."

I'm very lucky that I've got a husband who doesn't see me as a primary caretaker. He sees himself as a person who is just as responsible for raising the children as I am.

> "I see myself as a person who is great at problem-solving"

**So when did you first discover that you, personally, had some entrepreneurial talent?**

I don't know if I've got entrepreneurial talent. I don't really think about it. You don't suddenly wake up one day and go, "Oh, I'm an entrepreneur" because I think when you look at the term 'entrepreneur,' it depends on how it's defined.

I see myself as a person who is great at problem-solving, has strong tenacity, has phenomenal drive and is obsessive-compulsive because I think you have to be a little bit odd and a little bit obsessive to be successful.

I've always seen myself as a businesswoman. I've always seen myself as a business leader in later times in my business but I have certainly never sat down and had a conscious thought about being an entrepreneur.

**What is your approach to marketing and how did you get your name, and your company's name, out into the marketplace?**

You haven't really got a lot of money to spend on marketing because you're spending a lot on building stores, staff and infrastructure. Marketing is very difficult when you're younger.

We used every skill we had and every resource that we had. One of the resources was me. There weren't many businesses out there that were run by a woman and we used that in a PR capacity. Whenever we did promotions, we always did them loud and proud. They were always a bit quirky and a bit unique so people talked about them.

We continued to talk to our customers to see what their needs were. I think a lot of businesses out there don't do that. We did qualitative and quantitative research. Every six months, we would get a group of our customers in and show them new products and new marketing initiatives.

"The key thing is to understand your target market"

We have a vibe club, which is a million people that we actually send out different campaigns to and see what they think. So you do as much as you can in research before you start spending the big marketing dollars. Even today, considering the size of that business, we don't spend a fortune on marketing so every cent that we do spend has to be effective.

**What would your top tips be for effectively branding a business?**

The key thing is to understand your target market, then you can narrow your marketing effectively. We know our target market is mostly outdoors, so we go outdoors - billboards, radio, bus shelters. Those types of mediums are more effective to our target market.

The other thing is you need to understand your 'bull's eye.' Our 'bull's eye' is a girl called Zara. She's 25 years old. She shops at certain boutiques. Her friends are really important to her and she is on different social media. We have a long list of things that Zara does.

Once we understood who Zara was for us and our market, we could then market directly to her. So then we look at our marketing and ask, "Is this directed at Zara?"

## When did you know that it was time to think about franchising the brand?

We franchised very early at the Boost creation. It was really a solution to a problem. The problem was, "How do we grow really fast in a marketplace where we knew that the competitors would come in and swamp us? How do we do it safely and how do we do it in a way that we can get quality people on board who will help us grow?"

Franchising was the answer for us to be able to achieve our goals and succeed. It meant that we could confidently go out and sign a lot of leases and commit to a lot of deals, knowing that we had a pipeline of people, quality people, who could come in and run the stores with the vision that we had.

## How did you promote and sell your first few franchises?

It wasn't actually that hard. We found people came to us in the early days and even today, we have more enquiries for franchises than any other business in Australia. We had, at one point in our life cycle, only 7% of people who applied that actually got a franchise because there were so many people who wanted one. We were and we still are very strict about who comes into the business.

We had a list of 134 people waiting for stores. That wasn't one of our problems. We had other problems. That one wasn't one of them.

## So how did the brand evolve from start-up to how it is in the marketplace today? Is it similar or is it very different?

I think the values of the business and the vision of the business is the same as day one. The business is more robust. In the early days, I was the jack of all trades and trying to learn as quickly as I could. Now, we have experts in purchasing, experts in marketing, experts in legal and experts in accounting instead of me trying to work out how Excel spreadsheets work.

So the business has grown up. It was a young child learning to walk and learning how to do everything. It went through its adolescence. It went through its pimply stage where we got things wrong and sales went south for a while until we matured into the next phase, which was more of a mature business that is robust and built on a solid foundation.

**So what was your international expansion strategy?**

It was 2004 and we sat down as we did every six months and looked at how we actually needed to grow. We realised that the growth of Boost in Australia wasn't enough to maintain the growth that we wanted for the business.

So, we had to look at other shopping centres and other markets around the world. We did research on the wellness category and found that it was very strong and it wasn't just Australia, England and America that was struggling with obesity, it was many countries around the world.

So I went, in 2004, to an expo in Washington, D.C. to understand how the international market works. That was the first step to working out how to do it.

**What's been the biggest challenge you've had to face within the franchise business?**

There's not a single challenge that you face. I think it's constantly ensuring that the culture of the franchise network is strong but I'm happy to say that the research we do with our franchisees shows they're up in the 80-percentile, which is fantastic and apparently ten times above industry standards, which we're really proud of.

I think the challenge is just keeping open communication and the culture. It's not one of those problems where you say, "Okay, fix that. What's the next problem?" It's that constant, "Okay, how do we continue to work on the culture?"

"The franchisor must make sure that their business is profitable"

**So what is the most important thing or things you've learnt about successful franchising?**

That communication is very important. I think nine times out of ten, the reason franchisees get disgruntled and the franchisors get disgruntled is because they're not communicating effectively enough. If you're not communicating effectively enough, people will make up their own mind and it's always worse than the reality anyway.

**In your opinion, what are the most common mistakes that new franchisors or franchisees make?**

The franchisor must make sure that their business is profitable and robust enough to be franchisable. Sometimes people try and jump in too soon and they haven't really got the systems, processes or business model to be franchisable.

The other thing is that sometimes they're not good marketers. Some franchisors haven't got the strength they need in that area.

**So what do you believe are the essential qualities or attributes of a successful franchise system?**

The key thing is openness. Openness when things are going great and openness when things aren't going so great. I know in our business, that every franchisee can see everyone else's sales which helps with competition but it also helps people to benchmark against others so they know what's going on. That takes away a lot of miscommunication so people can see the transparency of the business.

Sometimes people's lives change. Great people in business have tragedies in their lives and then suddenly they're not focusing on their business but on their struggles. It's making sure that we can work with our partners to help them when they are struggling.

**So what advice would you give to someone who is thinking about investing in a franchise?**

Do your research. Ask a lot of the franchisees that are in that network what they think. Make sure that you do as much of your own research as possible. Don't rely on anyone else. The more research that you do on a business, the less risk there is.

**What stops people from being successful, from your perspective?**

People sometimes see a problem as unfixable while other people see it as a challenge. Some people see something as drama and other people see it as, "I could solve that. No problem."

I categorise people into two areas: Being averse or being the type of person who can soar. Being averse, to me, is someone who's a victim; everything bad happens to them, they're entitled. So, for example, "I've been in my job for ten years. Why don't I get a promotion?" They're always looking for other people to solve their problems, not solving their own problems, it's never their fault, it's always someone else's fault.

Then, there are people who can SOAR, people who are solution-based. The problem comes up and they ask, "How am I going to fix it?" Ownership: "It's my problem to fix." Accountability: "If it's up to me, it will be." Responsibility: Making sure that they can make it a reality.

"You need to have effectiveness to be successful."

**What do you believe are the essential qualities or personal attributes of a successful person?**
People who have all of the SOAR attributes mentioned in my last answer. People who aren't drama queens and just get on with it.

You find most highly successful people have an element of effectiveness and I think you need to have effectiveness to be successful. For you to actually get to the top, the focus that you have to give and the sacrifices you have to give to get there, are many.

**What do you think holds people back from achieving their goals?**
Mostly fear. I think that when someone asks you to do something or asks you to go somewhere, it's easier to say "No," because as soon as you say "No," that problem goes away or that challenge goes away. If you say "Yes," that means you have to face it and you have to attend to it and you have to do it. It's easier to say "No."

Also courage. Luckily, my husband and I are very similar with regard to courage. For us to have three children at home, sell our family home and put all that into the business; that took a lot of courage.

**How would you describe your own personal management style?**

I never yell at people. I don't think that achieves anything. I feel that I communicate very clearly. I actually expect people to do what they say they're going to do and I will create systems to monitor whether they do it or not.

> "Ensure that everyone who's on a journey is happy to be on that journey."

If I have a meeting, that meeting will always have an action plan and that action plan will always have a date. I do expect that person to achieve those dates. I would say I'm firm, fair and demanding but I am only demanding what they've already said they're going to do. I actually make my people accountable.

**What are your secrets to being such a successful businesswoman?**

I don't know if there are any secrets. I certainly think picking the right partner is an important one. I've got friends out there who could have achieved anything but because they married a man or woman who lives in fear saying, "Oh, no, we can't sell our home" or "We can't do that" or "No, don't leave your job because we won't be able to pay the school fees," they haven't achieved anything.

If that person, male or female, married someone else who said, "Yes, we can do it. We'll find a solution," then that person might have achieved more. So it's very difficult if your life partner isn't on the same path as you or has a different level of comfort regarding risk than you do.

I think that one of the key things is to ensure that everyone who's on a journey is happy to be on that journey.

**How do you stay focused and on track daily and long-term, especially when times do get tough?**

I find that the only time I ever get a little bit down is when I'm not doing anything. I think my journey in life is to be better and that is a better person, a healthier person. In business, I want to be the best I can be, so it's that innate drive for excellence.

> "Some people out there who are very coachable and some people that aren't."

**Who would you say has inspired you in the past?**

Inspired and encouraged by my husband Jeff. He's very talented and certainly what he's good at is the ability to make things happen; it's extraordinary. You have people like Jeff Harris who was an early friend and investor in the business.

I think from afar, you get inspired by people like Anita Roddick. I think that you have Hillary Clinton. People who can achieve more than they even expected they could achieve themselves.

**As a top businesswoman, a very successful one, what do you hope to inspire in others?**

It's an interesting journey you go on. In the year 2000, about 15 years ago, I was the girl saying, "How am I going to do this? What is debit or credit? How do I hire someone? What the hell is GST? What do you mean there's no GST on fruit juice?" and "Oh, my God, how am I going to work this out?" but now I am the person who is working it out.

I've got all of these lessons that I've learned in the last 15, 16 years. With my role in "Shark Tank," I'm coming across these baby businesses again and I'm going "Wow! That's right, I was there. That's right. I had that fear, I had that dream." When this guy I've invested in turns around and says, "I don't know how to hire someone," I say "Yep, no problem, I've been there."

I must admit I do get great joy out of it.

There are some people out there who are very coachable and some people that aren't. I was one of those ones that went, "Give me all the diamonds that you've got, Jeff Harris, and all these other business people and I'll pick them up and use them."

> "Success, for me, is love."

There are other people and they'll ask you a question and you'll give them an answer but you know they're not listening. So the joy comes from those people who not only listen but actually act on your advice and see the benefit of that.

**So what does success mean to you? How does someone achieve that or have more of it?**

There are definitely different things for different people at different times in their life. For me, success is having my family around and them getting along and them wanting to be with me as they're becoming their own little adults.

Success is, for me, to create and help guide my children to accomplish their greatest achievements. If that is for one of my children to be the best hippie he can be, that's fine. As long as he's the best at what he wants to do. Success is having a husband who, after 20 years, I adore. Success is having a great relationship with my mother.

I'm very lucky to have financial freedom. That one is taken away as a stress. Success is not necessarily for me having a bigger, better house or a bigger, better car. Success, for me, is love. That sounds corny, but it's true.

**What is the most important piece of advice anyone has ever given you?**

> "Fire quick, hire slow"

I can't recall one line of advice. One of the things that really helped the business in the early years was Jeff Harris talking about profit centres and dividing the business into sections to make people accountable for their own expenses. I found that there was something called the sinkhole or black hole of expenses that no one was accountable for. That was a time when the business really started to turn around and become incredibly profitable.

I suppose it's the classic line of, "Fire quick, hire slow" and making sure you have great people surrounding you at all times.

**What drives you to continue to grow even more?**
It's the curious mind. It's having variety in my life. I get great fun and joy out of what I do. I'm 50 this year and finally at 50, I have found life balance where I do yoga in the morning and I sometimes sneak off to the beach in the middle of the week. I still work but I do it in my own time and my own hours. For me, I've got a really great balance.

> "If you love life, life will love you right back."

**Is there a significant quote or saying that you live by or you've used quite often?**
One of the things that resonates with me is that if you love life, life will love you right back. What that means is

that if I look at life and say I'm really enjoying it and I'm really grateful for it, I'm grateful that my kids are healthy and I look at the good, not the bad, then I will find that that's what's reflected upon me.

If you look at life and see all the great things that are happening, suddenly, life is pretty good.

"Success is pushing those boundaries a bit further."

**What are some of your future plans and goals over the next five or ten years, personally or in business?**

"Shark Tank" has been an interesting journey and working with those businesses to try and make them as successful as they can possibly be. Continue to grow the Boost brand. Continue to watch my kids develop into gorgeous adults and just try to work out what I want to do when I grow up.

**What is your greatest passion in life?**

I think achieving success… That ties back to all the things I've said before. If we're doing the work and we're doing Boost, then success is achieving our goals. Success is pushing those boundaries a bit further and being a bit scared and still achieving it despite the fact that they were a little bit ambitious.

Success is making sure that I can get through my second series of yoga. That would be successful. I think success happens on many levels.

**How would you want to be remembered?**

As someone who has made a difference in Australian business. Someone who has inspired people to create a business and live their dream. Someone who wasn't necessarily given anything but achieved great things in business, which would then, hopefully, inspire other people to not look at what they haven't got but to actually look at what they have got and then continue just to do it.

I hope I'm remembered as someone who is kind.

*If you love life, life will love you right back.*

# CHAPTER 3

## SARAH ALLEN

Appliance Tagging Services

# CHAPTER 3

## SARAH ALLEN -
Appliance Tagging Services

*Just be confident. Confident in your ideas, confident in your instincts and just back yourself. Know that you can do it.*

Sarah Allen is the cofounder and general manager of Appliance Tagging Services. She is also secretary of the National Electrical Safety Testing Association, the peak body for the electrical safety profession in Australia.

Established by Sarah and her husband, Ainslie, in 2006, Appliance Tagging Services are an award winning franchise system regarded as

Australia's premier electrical test and tag provider.

ATS featured on BRW's Fast Franchises list for 4 years running and took out Smart Company's Top Franchisor Award in 2010 and the FCA Emerging Franchisor of the Year in 2011.

Heading up the PR, Sales and Marketing functions of the business, Sarah is responsible for brand development and national contracts. She also oversees the franchise network, assisting franchisees in establishing their businesses and driving sales locally.

An accomplished skier, yachtswoman and mother of two, Sarah focuses her energy on developing the business and, having written numerous articles on electrical safety, has become an active spokeswoman for the importance of safety in the Australian workplace.

**Can you tell us a little bit about yourself and your company?**
I grew up in Adelaide, a lovely place, and lived in Adelaide up until I was 23. I had a fabulous job with Colgate-Palmolive and in the 13 years that I was with Colgate I travelled around Australia and ended up in Melbourne where I met my husband and the rest, I guess, is history.

Our company is Appliance Tagging Services. We established the business in 2002 as part of our electrical contracting business which was based in Victoria. My husband is an electrician by trade and in 2004 we decided to franchise the business so I joined the business in 2006, after having a couple of children. We spent quite a lot of time developing the franchise model. When we decided we were ready to franchise and grant our first franchise in 2006 that was when I joined the business. So it was very, very exciting.

We're tracking really, really well. We've been going now for eight years. Our revenue is up year on year. Our average franchisee revenue is up nearly 30% on previous years, so that is just fantastic and we've been growing at about 40% per year over the last five or six years. So business is going from strength to strength.

**What do you think were some of the factors that contributed to your company's exciting growth?**

I think the biggest factor with our growth is that we identified a niche and we've really stuck to that niche over the past eight years. We identified that testing and tagging, whist not being terribly sexy or exciting, is an area of business that people have to comply with. It's regulated by government and people might not enjoy doing it, but they have to. So we are really focused on that.

We've really focused on investing in our systems, investing in the future, in our people, in our equipment, making sure that we're always growing. We are constantly reinvesting so that we are the best in the country and that we are exceeding what our clients want.

**So what are some of the most exciting changes you've experienced?**

I remember back in 2009, we had outgrown the office that we were in and we were in the privileged place where we owned our premises. We had people sharing desks and it was very, very squishy. It was very exciting when we actually put the second level on our office. We've now got to the point now where we're starting to get a little squishy again, so there may be a third level!

The most exciting thing that's happening is that we've been developing our own, proprietary testing equipment since 2006 and we're due to roll it out this year. So our franchise network is very excited, as are all of us in the support office. We should be fully rolled out by the end of the year. It's really, really exciting because that's going to give us the next big growth numbers as well. There's been a lot of planning and not only are we rolling out new equipment but we're completely changing our entire back end system as well.

"You find yourself working days and nights."

**What do you believe was your biggest sacrifice in getting the business off the ground?**

Time and money are the two biggest sacrifices anybody makes when they're getting their businesses off the ground.

You find yourself working days and nights. My kids were little so we would work all day, get home, have dinner with the kids, put them to bed and then work until midnight. Get up and do it all again the next day.

Any profit that was in the business, we reinvested straight back into it. I didn't draw a wage for years. That's just what you do in order to get ahead and make sure that you're growing something that's going to be sustainable.

"We engaged a franchise specialist."

**If there was one key area in management that you would do differently, what would it be?**

I would engage specialist people more quickly and not say, "I've got skills in that area, I can do that," and take so much on myself because in the end you do get burnt out. We engaged a franchise specialist and we worked with consultants in the development of our model but we had only one franchisee. We made the brave decision to put on a franchise development person and our business went from strength to strength following that.

> "Know that you can do it."

We rejigged our model a bit. We completely changed our operations manual. We did a whole bunch of things that we probably should have done early on. Engaging specialists and experts in their area will actually save you money in the long run and I wish we'd done it a bit sooner.

**What would you say has been the highlight for your business so far?**

There are two big ones. We were incredibly proud in 2011 to be the Franchise Council of Australia's Emerging Franchise System of the Year. It was a goal that we'd set ourselves five years earlier and it was set over a bottle of red, with a bit of a laugh, but then five years later, we actually achieved it. So that was just incredible and we were very, very proud of that.

And then two years later, in 2013, one of our franchisees was successful in Franchisee of the Year for less than two staff.

Those two recognitions of our system just really give us strength and confidence in what we're delivering to the network because we believe we have a fabulous system and that our franchisees are achieving success and it's just nice to have that verified.

**What tips would you give to other businesswomen who are getting into business?**

Just be confident. Confident in your ideas, confident in your instincts and just back yourself. Know that you can do it. We're our biggest enemies. We're the ones who are constantly in our mind putting up barriers and saying, "I can't do that." I speak to people who can give me ten reasons why they can't do something but only one why they can. If we just change our thinking around to, "Yes, I can do that" and "I know I can do it," and be a bit brave, I think that would be the biggest tip. Just take a punt, trust in yourself and go for it!

"We're really only as good as our team."

**When did you first discover that you had entrepreneurial talent?**

I don't think I'm particularly entrepreneurial. I know with our business this is very much a team effort. I do recall my parents gave me my Grade 2 school report a few years ago, which said that I was bossy in a group. I think they call it "leadership" now! But back in Grade 2, being bossy in a group was probably not the right thing to be. I believe that there's no such thing as an overnight success and there's no such thing as a leader who just makes everything happen themselves. It truly is with us; it's a team effort and we're really only as good as our team. And at the moment, we have a fabulous team.

**What is your approach to marketing and how did you get your name out into the marketplace?**

This has been a big challenge for us because testing and tagging is not terribly sexy. People don't wake up in the morning and say, "I'm going to go and engage someone to do testing and tagging today." It's not that exciting, so our biggest question was, "How do we position ourselves as experts within this field and how do we position ourselves as the most professional and the company that people will call when they need advice or a service provider or somebody that they can trust?"

"We have also leveraged relationships "

We then focused on our website and how much information we could put out there in order to establish our expertise. We wrote numerous articles for industry publications on electrical safety. It's an area of really great confusion and because the rules vary around the country, it then gave us an opportunity to clear up some of that confusion and really set ourselves up as the experts.

We have also leveraged relationships that we have with our key clients. We are a business-to-business system. Over time we've really been able to use referrals as a good way of getting our brand out there and I'd like to think that we're the most well-known brand in our field in Australia.

**What are your top tips for effectively branding the business?**
It's understanding where you sit in the marketplace, knowing your niche, knowing who your customer is and not trying to be all things to all people. It's really understanding where you sit then screaming that and making sure that whatever you're doing is consistent with that niche.

There are so many more services our guys could provide while they're on site. We could try really hard to be everything to everybody but we want to be known for one thing and doing one thing really, really well and that's what builds a brand.

**When did you know it was time to think about franchising the brand?**
That was 2004. We had, particularly with a number of national clients, the tyranny of distance and it was killing us. We were sending contractors from Melbourne to Cairns and over to Perth in order to service these clients. We had secured work and we were promising the world but not

delivering very much. So we had to think about a new business model, whether that was to employ people in each state or whether that was to come up with some other way.

We knew that we were really good at managing the relationship with national clients, winning that work and giving the client what they wanted but we also knew that if we franchised the business, our franchisees would be able to go and market their business locally and secure clients that we could never go and talk to because there are just so many people out there. So we thought, "This has got to be the best of both worlds, with a franchisee growing their business locally and us securing work nationally." So we thought we'd hit on something that was just a little bit different from what was already out there in the marketplace with franchising and I guess the proof's in the pudding. It's certainly been successful.

**How did you promote and sell your first few franchises?**

The first one came on a little bit quicker than we wanted it to. He's still with us now. He was a colleague of one of our former employees and he liked what he'd heard through this colleague. He came on board as our first franchisee and he is the most patient, wonderful man. The system that he joined, back in 2006, is so different to the system that exists now.

But apart from that, we've promoted through our own website, through newspaper advertisements, exhibitions, the Franchise Council website, SEEK Commercial and other sites. In regional areas, especially early on, newspaper advertisements worked really well. We are starting to get franchisees being referred to us by our current franchisees, which is fabulous.

> “We know what works”

**How did the brand evolve from start up until now in how you market?**

We’re just doing everything better. We’re not as hit and miss as we used to be. We know what works, so we know that a referral from a franchisee is far better than a cold enquiry. We’ll use an exhibition in a state where we need to strategically try and grant more franchises. So we’re certainly more strategic than we were early on when we were just looking for franchisees all over the country.

Because we had national clients, we instantly needed franchisees in Perth, Darwin, Hobart and Cairns. We were very lucky that our first franchisees were spread around the country and that they were also happy to travel. We’re more strategic and more targeted about how we market for our franchisees now.

> “Cash flow is one of the hardest things”

**What has been one of the biggest challenges you’ve had to face in the franchise business and how did you overcome it?**

There are two big things. Cash flow is one of the hardest things in any business and is especially so with our model. Our franchisees are paid, regardless of whether the client has paid us or not. Our support office does all of the back end of a franchisee’s business which means we do all of their invoicing and debt collection. We’re in control of the money but then that also has a huge cash flow risk at our end, so that’s been one of the hardest.

And the other one is just managing people’s expectations and the expectations of our franchisees. Regardless of whether we like it or

"It is all about the people!"

not, people come into a business with a certain set of assumptions and whether their assumptions are right or wrong, it's still what they assume and so it's really about trying to manage that expectation. The people aspect of franchising has been one of our really big growth curves. I'd like to think that we do it better than we ever have but I don't think any business out there can say that they've got it perfected. We can always improve.

**What is the most important thing you have learned about successful franchising?**

It is all about the people! It is about the people and their families and understanding what drives them. Everybody is different and what I think is fair and reasonable is not fair and reasonable to the next person. It's about understanding that.

**In your opinion, what are the most common mistakes new franchisors and franchisees make?**

I know early on we developed our system and had a whole bunch of people saying, "This is wrong with your system" and "Why don't you do this?" Especially early on, everybody that joined wanted to change the system. There is a temptation to say, "We'll change that little bit for you and then that little bit for you." Whereas we were quite focused on, "No, this is what the system is" and we've really stuck to our guns, which has been very good because we now have a scalable system that works for 10 franchisees right through to 200 franchisees. I think that it's really important to make sure that your system is scalable and that you don't fall into the trap of making

"Make sure that your system is scalable"

short-terms decisions that have short-term benefits. It's really got to be about, "Am I going to wake up in five years time and regret this decision? Do I need to think a bit more long term about this?" It might be the simple answer but sometimes the simple things aren't necessarily the right things to do.

"We are only as good as our worst-performing franchisee."

**What do you believe are the essential qualities or attributes of a successful franchise or franchise system?**

They have got to be great communicators. I think they've got to be full of 'people' people; staff who really enjoy engaging with people and who are passionate about their niche and the brand.

Franchisee selection. We are only as good as our worst-performing franchisee. I know that our franchisees get really upset if we put on a franchisee who doesn't meet their expectations. They get really, really upset because they see that as devaluing their business.

**What advice would you give to someone who's thinking about investing in a franchise?**

"Get the good, the bad and the ugly."

Do as much research as you possibly can. Speak to as many existing franchisees as you can, get the good, the bad and the ugly. There'll always be somebody who's unhappy and there'll always be somebody who's delighted. So, I think you've got to go into any business, thinking "Yes, there are going to be highs and lows, there are going to be challenges and there are going to be successes. Does the culture fit for me? Do the people fit for me? Is it an industry that I'm passionate about?" They need to understand that there are going to be highs and lows.

**From your perspective, what stops people from being successful?**

I think people focus on the negatives and that they are naturally risk-averse; that we don't really like to step outside of our comfort zone. Sometimes you just need to be brave, back yourself and give it a shot.

**What do you believe are the essential qualities or personal attributes of a successful person?**

I think they've got a really strong vision for the future and they surround themselves with people who are smarter than they are. They know where they want to go and they know the 'rough' steps for how to get there but they're smart enough to understand that they can't do everything themselves. They need to just surround themselves with people who have all those attributes that they don't have.

**What do you think holds people back from achieving their goals?**

They just don't believe in themselves. They don't give themselves the tools to be able to do it. They come up with excuses.

We've got a couple of franchisees who have set themselves goals and then 12 months later they haven't achieved any of them because they didn't actually do any of the actions that they'd set themselves. They say, "Well, I just didn't think I could do it, so I didn't do it."

**How would you describe your management style?**

I would say "open and quite flexible and adaptive." I'm more than happy to hear the good and the bad. I really like consulting with our team about different things because I know I don't have all the good ideas. Our team has certainly come up with lots of different ways of doing things that I would never have thought of, so I really like to get everybody involved.

> "I really like to get everybody involved."

**What are your secrets to being a successful businesswoman?**

A crazy amount of preparation, planning and prioritising. It is all about making sure that you get the stuff that needs to be done, done, and really just keeping on top of everything.

**How do you stay focused and on track daily and long term especially when times get really tough?**

You could say I'm in a good position or you could say it's a bad position in that I work with my husband, so we do tend to keep each other on track and what we've found is that when I'm down, he's up, and vice versa, so we do tend to give each other support. My children keep me on track because that really is the bigger picture. "What are we really doing this for?"

When times are tough, we really just get back to basics and go, "Right. What are we doing this for? What is the bigger picture?" In five years, are we going to look at this and say, "Yes, this was a disaster" or are we going to say, "Oh, goodness! That was just a blip"? So we try really hard to put things into perspective.

> "When times are tough, we really just get back to basics"

If it's not an issue in five years time, then let's not talk about it now. Let's just get over it.

"Everything can be overcome, the world doesn't end."

**Who would you say has inspired you in the past?**

Everybody says, "Richard Branson," but I think that's just because he really looks like he loves what he does. I find that really inspirational, that you can absolutely love what you do. You can have a heap of fun doing it and he's brave and makes really bold, but quite researched and calculated, decisions.

I also look to Janine Allis. I heard her speak recently and the journey that she went through just to have that perseverance in order to just keep going and keep backing herself gives you the courage to keep going.

Every time I listen to a speaker it makes me realise that we all have our ups and downs. That it is hard but nobody ever talks about the hard stuff. We all keep it close because we don't want to admit that sometimes things are hard. All of those speakers who are brave enough to say, "Well, this is my journey and these are the hard things but this is how we overcame them" are really inspirational!

"You've just got to really want it."

Everything can be overcome, the world doesn't end. I think I've often said that you go to industry meetings and everybody stands around telling everybody how fabulous life is but I liken it to ducks where, on the surface, everything is wonderful but underneath, we're all just paddling and trying to survive.

**As a top successful businesswoman, what do you hope to inspire in others?**

That you can do anything you put your mind to. You've just got to really put your mind to it. You've just got to really want it. If you don't want it and you're not 100% committed to it, you'll never, ever achieve it. It really is about putting your heart and your soul into something because only then will you achieve it.

"Always start with the end in mind."

**What does success mean to you? How does one achieve it or have more of it?**

I think working fewer nights [chuckles]! Working fewer nights is good. That the cash is flowing, that's also good!

Our franchisee's achievements, our staff satisfaction. It's not necessarily about us achieving our goals. We've certainly set goals for our business but I get great satisfaction in seeing our franchisees succeed. In some cases, they've created whole new lives for their families, which is wonderful to watch. So that really drives success for me, rather than just the personal stuff. Although working fewer nights is quite nice.

**What is the most important piece of advice anyone has ever given you?**

"Always start with the end in mind." What does it look like when the business is grown up? Make decisions that, when you have 200 franchisees, are still going to be the right decision. Make sure that your systems are scalable and that you're not making short-term ones and that you're always trying to design a system that will grow with your number of franchisees.

**What drives you to continue to grow?**

It's franchisee achievements. We've got a fantastic model and I know we can take our model overseas. We can share our successes with other people and that's what drives us to keep going.

"No excuses, just service."

**Is there a significant quote or saying that you live your life by?**

I've got two. The best boss I ever had, when I worked at Colgate, once said to me, "Don't worry about the things you can't change." Sometimes we just get caught up in those little things that we can't change and we just stew over them whereas we should just say, "Right, I can't change it. Let's just move on."

The other one is what we have within our support office, which is "No excuses, just service." That's what our service team, our operational team live by. Neither a franchisee nor a client want an excuse, they just want service, so how are we going to do that?

**What are some of your future plans and goals for the next five or ten years?**

Well, it's definitely international expansion. So, we're in the fortunate position that the Australian standards that our industry is governed by also apply in New Zealand and a very similar standard is operational in the UK. In the U.S. and Canada, there's nothing like what we do but it's governed in the UK, New Zealand and Australia so international expansion is definitely on the cards.

**What is your greatest passion in life?**

It's my family. I'm fortunate that I get to work with my husband. It can be good and bad but we are sharing this together, which I think is wonderful. I do think that it is a great example to our children that we can create something together.

We're small enough at the moment in that franchisees are like a family. I know them all. I know their wives names and I know their kids names. We get to go out for dinner and I think that's beautiful. So, certainly as we grow, that's less and less likely to happen and that will be a bit sad because it's quite nice to feel like we are one big family.

**How do you want to be remembered?**

Dedicated to and supportive of our team, whether that be franchisees or the people in our support office. Hardworking and, I guess, just inspiring.

I look at my kids and I think, "If I can inspire them to go and do something a bit brave, and a bit risky, then I think I've done my job." Also, to make some fairly strategic decisions before they do that but to go and do it and to really back themselves.

*You've just got to really want it. If you don't want it and you're not 100% committed to it, you'll never, ever achieve it.*

# CHAPTER 4

## LESLEY GILLESPIE
Bakers Delight

# CHAPTER 4

## LESLEY GILLESPIE -
Bakers Delight

*It's often the baby steps. You take one baby step, that worked, then you take another and another and before you know it, you've arrived, so to speak.*

Lesley's first full time job was as a secondary school teacher at Footscray High School, starting in 1978, after completing her BSc Hons and Dip Ed at Monash University in 1977. In 1980 she started Bakers Delight in

Hawthorn, Victoria with two other partners, Roger Gillespie and Gary Stephenson. She gained bakery experience from working extensively in the Old Style Bread Centre chain (later to become Brumby's) whilst also studying at university.

In 1983, Lesley and Roger bought out their partner, Gary Stephenson, and they started to develop the Bakers Delight chain which is now the largest national chain of bakeries in Australia with over 700 bakeries operating throughout Australia, New Zealand and Canada. From 1989 to 1999, Lesley also worked part-time as a secondary school teacher at Loreto Mandeville Hall in Toorak Victoria.

Currently, Lesley is Executive Director and Joint CEO of Bakers Delight Holdings Ltd. Her achievements include being a finalist in the Prime Minister's Award for Community Partnerships – Bakers Delight and the Breast Cancer Network of Australia 2004, Boroondara Citizen of the Year 2002 (shared with her husband Roger) and being awarded an OAM in 2006 in recognition of her work in business and philanthropy.

Lesley continues to expand her interest in retail with involvement in the grocery outlet chain based in Victoria NQR where she serves on its board as well as being a joint owner.

Apart from the ongoing and active partnership with Bakers Delight and BCNA, Lesley is also a patron of the Margaret Pratt Foundation which supports research into transplanted organ rejection.

In November 2013, Lesley was awarded a Fellowship from Monash University in recognition of her contribution to business and the community.

**Could you tell us a little bit about yourself and your company?**

I basically grew up in suburban Melbourne. I spent most of my primary school years at Glen Waverly State School and then my high school years were spent at Glen Waverly High School. I left at year 12, in 1972, and then spent five years at Monash University, where I did a science degree majoring in chemistry and genetics followed by an honours year in chemistry and then a diploma of education.

My first job was at a local hardware store. It's now defunct. It was called McKewens and that was when I was in year 9. I had different jobs in retail throughout school and university. Bakers Delight was the first business I owned and that started in 1980. The way it started is quite interesting but in the 1970s, there was a niche created whereby small hot bread shops started to proliferate. Big bakeries, at the time, were prohibited by law from baking on a Saturday and a Sunday so these smaller hot bread shops sprung up where they were able to bake on Saturday and Sunday. The Australian population responded incredibly positively to this and some would say Bakers Delight was an evolution of that.

There was Roger, my husband, myself and a good friend, Garry Stephenson, who was also a baker. With all of the confidence of 20 something-year-old people, we borrowed money from family, as the banks weren't interested in us. We then set up the first Bakers Delight in Glenferrie Road, Hawthorn, which is an inner suburb of Melbourne, and I can proudly say we are still in Glenferrie Road in Hawthorn.

In 1982, Garry told us that he would like us to buy him out. His true love was mathematics and he went back to that and did further study and then made his own way in his career. We are where we are now because of that one little bakery in Glenferrie Road in Hawthorn.

**Tell us about the company's current position, how are things tracking and what the vision for the business is.**

Well currently, we are operating in every state in Australia. We also have bakeries in New Zealand and Canada. We will be going to Connecticut in the United States, just about 40 minutes drive from New York City in a nice upper middle class family area. So that is pretty exciting. The US expansion hasn't been released on the website yet. We have just under 600 bakeries in Australia, 30 plus in New Zealand and 80 plus in Canada. We will be adding another 10 bakeries in Canada this year and we will be doing the same in Australia, so we are still in growth. The population in Australia is growing and we are moving with that and finding opportunities for our franchisees.

**What do you think are some of the factors that contributed to your company's exciting growth?**

When our bakeries are well run they are very profitable. When we first started franchising, in early 1989, we structured it so that our current bakery managers could become the franchisees; that all worked nicely. We found once the bakery managers had focus and skin in the game and were able to capitalise on profit, the profit grew 30% almost overnight. We then had all of their relatives, their friends, their bank managers and their accountants just lining up wanting to buy a franchise business from us. We could grow because everyone wanted to be part of it.

**What would you say are some of the most exciting changes you've experienced?**

We're so excited about going to Canada. Growing when it's been tough in retail, having good growth. We've got good growth at the moment in our existing bakeries. We've got some double digit growth in bakeries that are over 20 years old and they are still growing. I find that incredibly exciting.

"You just do it."

**What do you believe was your biggest sacrifice in getting the business off the ground back in those early days?**

You just don't think of it as a sacrifice. We had two little children and we needed to provide for them. We needed to have a home and we wanted to have enough money so we could make choices about where to send our children to school. You just do it. I never thought I had to make a sacrifice. I never felt at any stage in our married life that I went without.

**If there was one key area in management that you would do differently, what would it be?**

You can never wind back the clock but it would be to wait until I could get good people around me. Don't compromise and say, "Oh yeah, they will do." Hire strategically.

"Don't compromise. Hire strategically."

Plan better for the future so we have a constant flow of young people who want to be franchisees and young people who want to work corporately so they forge their careers through our organisation.

**What would you say has been the highlight of your business so far?**

Still being in business is a pretty good highlight after 35 years. Still expanding after 35 years is also really exciting and a highlight. And the growth in the bakeries – one which comes to mind is Mount Waverly, which is a nice family area in the eastern suburbs of Melbourne. This bakery is experiencing phenomenal growth, it's fantastic and the Mount

Waverly shopping centre hasn't changed a bit. I find that really exciting.

> "They've done the work but we've given them the opportunity."

I also find it a highlight when we take in a young person. Often, there is a reason why they left school at a very early age but they're hard working and want to make something of their lives and we put them through our franchisee training. We call it 'Fresh Franchisee Training.' We give them an opportunity to prove themselves and help them go into their own bakery and just see them fly. I really find that a highlight.

Knowing here they are, say five years on, franchisees who have a successful business and they continue to be successful. They've done the work but we've given them the opportunity.

**What tips would you give to other businesswomen who are getting into business right now?**

I would give this to a businessman as well. If you want to start off a business from an entrepreneurial perspective, everything takes twice as long and costs twice as much. Just be prepared for the long hard slog.

If a person wants to go into business and they've got a good idea and they are prepared to sell that idea then I say, "Go for it."

**When did you discover you had entrepreneurial talent?**

Well, I don't know. I wasn't the kind of kid that had their own business mowing lawns, although that is what my husband did as a young stud. I just think that perhaps because I met him and was attracted to him because of his fearlessness, I have a degree of fear that I could fall over or stumble and I could make a mistake. I'm not fearless all of the time but I was prepared to have a go so I guess I discovered my courage in my 20s.

It's often the baby steps."

It's often the baby steps. You take one baby step, that worked, then you take another and another and before you know it, you've arrived, so to speak.

**What is your approach to marketing and how did you get the Bakers Delight name into the marketplace?**
We are in a different kind of situation to some other businesses because we are in high street retail. People see us. So from my perspective, the best marketing is a vibrant environment in our bakery, fantastic products, the beautiful aroma of bread pervading the atmosphere and happy, efficient, smiling shop staff. That's what will stop someone walking along the street to look to their right and say, "Hmm" or walk to their left and say, "I might go in there." That's what will attract customers to the counter if you're in a shopping centre.

So as we have grown, we now have a marketing department but these smart people we've got in our marketing department will tell you, no matter how good their campaign is, no matter how clever the TV commercial is, no matter how innovative it is, if you don't have your franchisees on board, it adds up to nothing. So we have got to get it right in the bakery.

Bakeries that have grown the best are where we have got a committed franchisee, who embeds them self in the local community, whether that is by providing products for the local netball or football clubs or the aged care home. They become embedded in that community and the TV ads and other advertising just add to it.

"Branding is the people"

**What are your tips for effectively branding a business?**

To brand a business, make sure that you know what you're doing. Branding is the people so make sure you've got the best people and make sure your business is something simple so people can understand it.

**When did you know it was time to think about franchising the brand?**

As I said, we opened one bakery in 1980 and one became two, two became three and by 1987 we had 13 bakeries that Roger and I were running. For each bakery that we opened, the profits were less and the sales were less. That was the law of diminishing returns and we felt, "Oh my God, there has just got to be a better way. We needed a way of linking our bakery managers' accountability and responsibility with their salary, the profits and sales growth." At that time in the 80s, Australia had an influx of American franchises such as Kentucky Fried Chicken, Pizza Hut and McDonald's and they were able to expand. Roger and I thought this principle of franchising could be what was needed. And it was. It worked.

**How did you promote and sell your first franchises? Obviously it came from the in-house managers as you said earlier.**

What we did to start off with, because our bakery managers had no money, was "rent" the business to them with a franchise agreement drawn up by our solicitors with every 'I' dotted and 'T' crossed. They eventually paid us back and then they owned the business. As I mentioned earlier, when these business are run well, they're profitable and their friends, their relatives, their bank managers, our friends, our relatives and our bank managers were then lined up to buy a business.

**How did the brand evolve from start up to how you market now?**

There is 2% that goes to marketing as part of the franchise agreement. That money is spent on behalf of the franchisees. It can be anything from buying TV ads, which are incredibly expensive, through to upgrading and providing uniforms, through to a whole set of new bread tins and new bread racks. We can do a lot of whole lot of things with that marketing fund.

We now have a marketing calendar and it is tied in to the season or occasion. Easter is very big for us as is Christmas, back to school, Australia day and so on and we have a three week campaign for each of these occasions. Those franchisees who are on board with the campaign can really make the most of it. We're not on TV the whole time, we are on TV part of the time and we have radio ads and organise events during campaigns. It has to be with the input of the franchisee. Whatever works, we will do. If someone comes up with a good idea, we will do it.

**What has been the biggest challenge you've had to face in the business and how did you overcome it?**

The biggest challenge continues to be finding good franchisees, finding franchisees who are prepared to follow the system. That's an ongoing challenge and I'm sure every franchised business would say the same.

A big challenge was when a number of disgruntled ex-franchisees made a number of false and public accusations about us, which precipitated an ACCC investigation but we came out clean. So it was this and we still have these websites, Bakers Delight lies or BD lies where people can vent their pain. So that's not nice but it's there and it's a challenge if you're in business. I'm sure there are hate websites for almost any retail business out there.

> "We focus on the gross sales and profit."

When new franchisees come in, we let them know about this. The franchise code is terrific, it is very strict. The disclosure documents tell potential franchisees everything about Bakers Delight, warts and all, so when they become part of the network, they know.

**What is the most important thing you've learned about existing franchisees?**

From a franchise perspective, the business needs to be run so the franchisees make money. It's all about the franchisee profits and that's' how we run our business. We focus on the gross sales and profit.

**In your opinion, what are the most common mistakes new franchisors and franchisees make?**

From the outside and looking in at new franchisors, a lot of them think that because they've got a business they can franchise it but the business doesn't actually make enough money to franchise. The franchisee needs something out of it as well so you have to have a system that actually makes good money for the franchisee.

> "Some franchisees think it's going to be easier than it really is"

Every franchisee is an individual and they're all different. Some franchisees think it's going to be easier than it really is, even though you tell them. In their training it says, "This is going to be the most difficult thing you ever do." It's not until you do it that you realise that it is difficult, especially in our system, as it does require hands on involvement. Obviously, you can't be at your bakery 24/7 but you need to have the skills if the baker rings in sick or a shop person rings in sick. Sometimes you are the one to replace them on that day.

"If you are a part of a franchise, the likelihood of you failing is greatly reduced."

**What do you believe are the essential qualities and attributes of the successful franchisor or franchisee system?**
One, that they put the profits of the franchisee ahead of those of the franchisor and everything else follows that.

**What advice would you give someone who is thinking about investing in a franchise?**
Do your homework. Absolutely do your homework. Look at what you as a potential franchisee are interested in and investigate! There's a whole host of franchises out there, so do your homework and understand what's involved.

But typically, if you are a part of a franchise, the likelihood of you failing is greatly reduced. It's not reduced to zero of course but it is reduced.

**From your perspective, what do you think stops people from being successful?**
Perhaps they don't set their goals high enough. Some people are working at a certain level and a certain role and it suits them, so I call that being a success. For example, I'm sure in hospitals you will find nurses who've always been a nurse in a particular ward. They just love it and they continue to do it. I would say that that is a very successful career and a successful life.

But if you're unsuccessful, it's because you hate your job or you're not prepared to get out and work hard. I think it's the person them self that stops them from being successful especially in Australia; we've got a fantastic country where the sky is basically the limit.

"You have got to be passionate"

**What do you believe are the essential qualities or personal attributes of a successful person?**

Well, they're committed to whatever they're doing and they are passionate about it. You don't have to be in business. I gave you the nurse example. It doesn't matter.

The other day I had a dog bite me and my arm swelled up and I had to go to the doctor. Well, there's a nurse there who has been there for a very long time and she recognises me. I know she just loves her job. Once every two years I go and get this check-up and she takes blood from me. It's a small thing but she recognises me every time and she says hello and you can tell that this person has had a very successful career. So the point I'm making is, I think you have got to be passionate, you've got to be prepared to work hard and enjoy what you're doing.

**What do you think holds people back from achieving their goals?**

Somehow they must get stuck in a rut where they're doing stuff they don't like. They don't have the courage to resign and try something else.

**How would you describe your own management style?**

I'm probably not the right person to ask, maybe you should ask the people who've been reporting to me for years and years and years. I know that things will get done. There are shifts and changes all of the time. If there's a new person reporting to me, I want to know everything, just so that I know they're on the right track. I let people get on with doing the job, especially the ones who have been with me for a long time. I know that they know how to do the job. I meet with them once a week or once a fortnight. We've got a to-do list, work in progress, and they just get on with doing it and the results will show.

"I focus on what has to happen in the long term."

**What are your secrets to becoming or being a successful businesswoman like yourself?**
I don't think it is all luck. Perhaps I'd say a bit of luck and being in the right place at the right time. Good work ethics. My parents certainly instilled that.

**How do you stay focused and on track daily as well as long term, especially when those times do get tough in business?**
Well, I come to work every day. I have things that I need to do every day and things that I need to do every week. Obviously, I have holidays and time off. I travel a great deal to visit bakeries, so thank God for Microsoft Outlook.

I focus on what has to happen in the long term. For any business, you need to be growing long term. So the light on the hill is to be the world's best fresh bread retailer. I love it when I walk into a bakery and the floors and the counters are sparkling, I can smell the bread and the staff have their name badge on and they are smiling. The bread quality is exceptional and I can see that light on the hill glowing brightly. But sometimes that doesn't happen and I walk into a bakery and I see dirty things, marketing not up properly, grumpy people without name tags behind the counter and poor quality bread and that light on the hill dims. But that's the challenge. That's the challenge to keep going.

**Who would you say has inspired you in the past?**
I would say my mother and father. Definitely my mother. They were the ones who instilled values in my brother and me so they have been my inspiration.

"Don't give up, just keep on."

**As a top successful businesswoman, what do you hope to inspire in others?**
To succeed in whatever someone wants to do.

**What does success mean to you and how does one achieve it or have more of it?**
Success is obviously having a business that's growing, a business that's profitable but it's also based on the people. I mentioned earlier that we have a number of young people in our system and when I see those people succeed, I feel success. They make me feel as though we are going to be successful. We have got a number of young franchisees who've come through our system, they were originally headed off the rails but now they are respected business people. So that's what success means to me.

**What was the most important piece of advice anyone has given you?**
I guess don't give up, just keep on.

I think it was a Dominos Pizza ad when my son, who is now 35 but was in his early 20s or late teens, was delivering pizzas and the young lad goes to the door and the older man says, "That's great. Here's the 20 bucks," and the young man says, "What about a tip?" and the older man replies, "Oh! Sorry, Son. Work hard and be nice to your mother."

That's the tip. Work hard and be nice to your mother. I said to Roger, "That's the best ad ever" and I'm still talking about it. It really appealed to me. That's a pretty good bit of advice. If you work hard and are nice to your mother, life's pretty good.

"If you're not growing, you're going backwards."

**What drives you to continue to grow even more?**

If you're not growing, you're going backwards. The decisions that Roger and I make, even though we've got a fantastic team around us and we could go away hiking for eight weeks and we wouldn't be missed, affect the longevity of Bakers Delight. We have nearly five hundred franchisees who've invested their life savings with us. We have to be moving the business forward and growing otherwise they won't be growing.

**Is there a significant quote or saying which you live your life by?**

Well, it's not work hard and be nice to your mother but that's how I want my son to live. Work hard and be nice to your mother. Which he does and he's nice to his mother. There isn't really one significant quote, there are a whole lot of those little sayings like, 'Good luck comes to those who work hard' but I just get on with doing things.

"I just get on with doing things."

**So what are some of your future plans and goals for the next 5 to 10 years, and that can be personal or business of course?**

I mentioned earlier on that we are moving into the US, so that's very exciting to develop that market. We will continue our development in Canada and obviously Australia and New Zealand as well so we are in a growth phase. There will be more Bakers Delight bakeries opening in those four countries. I have a new little granddaughter and she is seven months old so it would be nice to spend some time with her.

Continue to grow Bakers Delight. That's my plan.

**What is your greatest passion in life?**

Obviously my family. Our son and daughter and our son-in-law. They're all involved in Bakers Delight and they all started on the bakery floor. They all hold senior positions now and they are positions that they've earned not been given because of their surname. It's fantastic for me to be able to say that they love Bakers Delight as much as I do.

I mentioned earlier how good it is to see franchisees become successful business people in their own right. That gives me great joy and also the fact that we're providing a great product to our customers; a great healthy product that has been around for a long time. I think we are lucky to be in a business where the product we sell is a staple and not only our customers but also our bakers, our shop staff, our franchisees and the people who work at the office absolutely love our bread and love our products. So we're blessed that that's what we do rather than something else.

**How would you like to be remembered?**

As the person who gave jobs to people. We employ a lot of people in our bakeries, so that's providing employment for Australians, Canadians, New Zealanders and Americans.

*If you're not growing,
you're going backwards.*

# CHAPTER 5

## TINA TOWER
Begin Bright

# CHAPTER 5

## **TINA TOWER -**
Begin Bright

*I've been so organised my whole life, everything I have has had a plan and a goal.*

At work

Not your ordinary Gen-Y female, Tina started her first business at the age of 20 and by the time she hit 30 had built and sold 2 businesses, completed a degree, got married, had two children and started in the challenging world of building a national franchise network. Half way through a primary teaching degree she saw a gap in the private education market and created her own tutoring centre straight away. Naivety was bliss! Finishing university two years later, Tina decided she loved being in business and could touch children's lives on a more individual level through her school readiness and primary tutoring centre than in a school so decided to make her life in business.

As children were coming in for tutoring with mostly reading problems, Tina began to develop a school readiness program that was designed to form a solid foundation and love of learning so that problems never occurred once at school. This is where Begin Bright was born. To fit it around having a family, Tina began licensing the Begin Bright program in 2009 and converted it to a franchise system in 2011. Three years in and Begin Bright has launched 13 franchises throughout NSW, VIC and QLD with plans to expand nationwide in 2014.

Tina was the 2012 winner of the My Business Awards for Women in Business and Begin Bright won the National Overall Winner for Commitment to Excellence. In 2013 Begin Bright took out the Australian Small Business Champion Awards for Educational Services and the Telstra Australian Young Business Woman of the Year in 2014.

Tina has been featured in The Australian, Daily Telegraph and 7 News, The Financial Review, The Australian, Today Tonight and Wake Up on Channel 10 and is passionate about inspiring and giving opportunities to young entrepreneurs. Tina also works with The Hunger Project and is determined to see the end of chronic hunger in her lifetime. Begin Bright is passionate about education across the world and is building a school in Laos with the Room To Read charity, in 2016.

At home

Always feeling the need to live a full life and play a bigger game, Tina married a very handsome man at 21 and had her first child at 24 followed by her second son a year later. Lucky to have a very supportive husband who shares parenting and household duties as well as working, it makes the balance easier to achieve. Now at 31 years old, she's feeling the truth in the adage of it taking 10 years to create an overnight success.

> "We're right on that really high growth trajectory."

Tina's mission in life is to run fantastic companies that make people happy and confident, keep a happy husband, be a wonderful mother to two gorgeous boys and travel the world and experience the best life possible. She has started a blog, The Juggling Act, designed for women who grapple daily with the guilt and feelings of inadequacy that come with running a great company and still being a present and valuable parent. In the testament to living what you preach, Tina has just moved from Sydney to an acreage North of Byron Bay for a great work/life balance and encourages everyone to let their own light shine.

**Tell us a little bit about yourself and your company**

I grew up in Sydney. I am 31 years old and I've been a business owner forever. I've never had a full-time job. When I finished school, I started a business degree at uni. I got to the end of that first year and I was told that I wasn't suited to the business world and I should find something a little bit more suited for my personality. Then I went into a primary teaching degree because that's what happy, bubbly girls are supposed to do, apparently. I was two years into my teaching degree when I started my first tutoring centre.

**Can you tell us about the company's current position and how things are tracking? What's the vision for the business?**

We've been going four years and we're right on that really high growth trajectory at the moment. Last year we doubled in franchise size from nine to 18 and this year we're aiming to add an additional 15. Our ultimate goal is to have 100 centres operating by 2018. That also means that our support office team is growing rapidly. We're in quite an exciting time.

"Change has been an absolute constant for us"

**What do you think were some of the factors that contributed to this growth?**

We have a really great business model. I think that's a pretty key ingredient that you need to start with. We've got really great core programs. It means that someone can come in and implement it in a really professional way, whether they are owners that have an educational background or not, they can still come in and use our business model and have a good lifestyle while being a business owner.

**What are some of the most exciting changes you've already experienced?**

Change has been an absolute constant for us; I think that's the way with any young company. Now that we're in our fourth year we're trying to slow down a little bit on the big changes. For a while we were trying to find our feet in the franchising market. Being quite young and female I think that a lot of the franchising idols that I had, had a very different way of running a system than what I wanted to do. We had to trial and test a lot of things to find who we wanted to be. Now that we know who we are as a company and how we want to operate, that makes it much easier. I think the most exciting change is just seeing the franchisees grow their businesses. Seeing their lifestyle change from people who have gone from full-time work into running their own business is a joy to watch.

"We made the decision early on not to take outside investments."

**What do you believe was your biggest sacrifice in getting the business off the ground?**

We made the decision early on not to take outside investments. We wanted to grow the business organically. Begin Bright was actually started in 2008 and we then started franchising in 2011. We started by redrawing $100,000 from our mortgage and then we got another $100,000 in a loan from my parents, which I thought was an absolute fortune at the time. But it went really quickly on simple things like graphic designing the website, the legalities and all the basics. About nine months after we started, we nearly ran out of money. We grew really quickly and we hit all of our targets but we just had to keep pumping a lot into the business. I had a call from our accountant and she told us we needed to slow down the growth so that we could just sit tight for a while and bank some of the money or move out of our house. We made the decision to move out of our lovely four-bedroom house and for seven weeks we lived very glamorously with a mattress on the floor in my mum's house before we were able to move into a granny flat. We were there for the next two years living off $200 a week after the rent was paid, which was quite a sacrifice and quite tough on our kids at that age. At that stage they were two and three years old. My husband made massive sacrifices, especially when our children were real babies, so that I was empowered and able to do what I wanted to do, which is supportive but it allowed us to pump everything back into the business, which is what built it to where it is now, so it was a worthy sacrifice.

"For seven weeks we lived very glamorously with a mattress on the floor.

**If there was one key area in management you would do differently, what would it be?**

I would love a bigger management team so we were not so stretched all of the time. We do as much as we can with the resources available and we do leverage that to its maximum.

"You can't please everybody 100% of the time."

The other thing I would do differently is not to take everything so personally. I know I did that way too much in the early days but I'm getting better at it now. You can't please everybody 100% of the time which is what my ultimate goal was. When I started franchising I was told that was really naïve but I truly believed that I could create a system where everyone was happy 100% of the time. The reality of that is that it just can't be done.

**What would you say have been the highlights so far?**

We've had a lot. I think one of my biggest highlights was at our franchise conference last year. We arranged for all of the owners to go swimming with dolphins. Franchising can be a bit of a thankless industry, so it was a great moment for me to see all of the owners just standing there absolutely beaming and celebrating their Begin Bright businesses.

I think the other highlights are our awards. We've won the Australian Small Business Champions, Franchise Council of Australia Awards and most recently I was awarded the Telstra Young Business Woman of the Year award, which was a 10-year goal, so that was beyond exciting for me.

"I think being a woman in business is a bit trickier."

**What tips would you give to other businesswomen who are getting into business?**

I think being a woman in business is a bit trickier than being a man in business. There are still a lot of the social expectations that we have to live by and that are in the back of our minds a lot. I think you have to make sure that your expectations actually match the reality of what you want to create as well. I think too many people have a really romantic notion of business and then when they get into it they don't actually want to put in the hard work because it's taking time away from their families. I find women, generally, suffer more than men from 'mother guilt'. You really need to make sure that you have the emotional capacity to support and handle both the family and the business. I think once you've got that, you find your conviction and self-belief. Be bold and go for it.

**When did you first discover that you had entrepreneurial talent?**

I don't have one of those stories where I was five and doing the lemonade stand. I never really knew what I wanted to do. I tried all sorts of things in high school but I always knew I wanted to live a life less ordinary. I went to my first Robert Kiyosaki seminar when I was 16 and Anthony Robbins from when I was 17 and bought my first investment property when I was 18. I always knew I didn't want an ordinary life of being an employee and having the standard things that happen to you. I wanted to create something but I didn't quite know what that was. I tried a few things first before I found my feet and then once I found education and the education industry at 20, I absolutely loved it.

**What is your approach to marketing and how did you get your name out into the marketplace?**

Our approach to marketing is really to be there and everywhere at all times. We've always leveraged as much as we can from the resources we had and by that I mean following a really super tight budget. We did everything that didn't cost a lot of money. I find that with 'high-budget'

> "We did things that required effort but not a lot of capital."

marketing, you don't have to put a lot of effort in, you just have to put a lot of money in but the strategy we used in Begin Bright required a lot of time and effort but didn't require a lot of capital. That was what worked the most for us and that was PR and PR and lots of PR and being an absolute pain in the ass to journalists and emailing them and sending them things all of the time so that we could, in the early days, appear to be a much bigger company and have a lot more credibility than we had earned already. With local marketing, instead of taking out newspaper ads, we would blow up helium balloons and just go to all the day-care centres and parks and hand them out to all of the children. All of the parks and the walkways were just a sea of our Begin Bright logo balloons. We did things that required effort but not a lot of capital.

**What are your top tips for effectively branding the business?**

Know very clearly where you stand so that you can communicate that effectively. As I said before, you can't be all things to all people. You've got to work out exactly who your target market is and what your brand stands for and that's who you communicate with. Have a really clear image, in terms of your logo and the colours that you're using. As your business grows, your image is everywhere and it's really difficult to change later on. You've got to be quite set on your image before you start scaling up. Have a name that's simple and relates to your customers because people need to Google it. They need to talk about it, so it needs to be a simple, relatable name.

**When did you know that it was time to think about franchising the brand?**

When we started franchising we'd been licensing first. I created the Begin

Bright school readiness program initially, so it was just for little people. After we saw a lot of kids that were struggling at school, I created the school readiness program so children can learn and love learning in a really awesome, effective way before they actually start school. Initially it was just to sell as a license to other teachers so they were able to teach on their own. What we found was that people needed a lot of business support. They knew that I ran successful tutoring centres and wanted to have help in this area. As a licensee, it wasn't really effective. We were really in the stage where we either had to keep it as it was designed and just accept how people were going to run their businesses using our programs or take a little bit of that control and have the consistency across the board and start franchising Begin Bright. Those were the two choices we had and we chose the franchising option.

"I've been so organised my whole life"

**How many licensees did you have before you went into franchising?**
We had 25.

I've been so organised my whole life, everything I have has had a plan and a goal. When we started licensing, we had no plans to go into franchising at all and our licenses were very cheap. They started off at $2,000 a year for the program. By the time we got franchising, they were $8,000 for the year. When we changed to the franchising model, which is offering a lot more support so you have to charge accordingly, we didn't actually convert any of our licensees to franchisees. We started from scratch, again.

**How did you promote those first few franchises?**
We started off with a lot of PR and a lot of educational publications. In

the beginning, we sold franchises only to people who were teachers. We have now changed that model. We sell franchises to anyone with the right attitude and they can employ the teachers.

**How's the brand evolved from start up to how you market now?**

It's hugely differently. As I said before, we were aiming for teachers but now we're getting a lot more owners who are really great individuals but don't have an educational background. They're more focused on the business side of things and are employing the teachers in each of the centres.

**What has been one of the biggest challenges you had to face in the franchise business and how did you overcome it?**

At the end of last year we made the biggest change that we've ever had in our system. We went from a fixed-franchise model into a royalty model. We knew it was going to be a huge challenge for our existing franchisees and it was something that I spent over a year on, weighing up the pros and cons of both models and where we wanted to be in the future. I had to make sure I was going to make the right decision for everybody involved. It was challenging having to stand at our conference and deliver that news then manage that kind of aftermath and handle all of the emotions that come with that.

"You've got to have a clear conviction all of the time."

**What is the most important thing you have learned about successful franchising?**

You've got to have a clear conviction all of the time. You can't keep everyone happy all of the time, try as you might. I think we need to have really well thought out decisions with

100% conviction so that when new things are implemented we know straight away that we're doing the right thing by the greatest number of people as possible and we can live with those decisions.

"There has to be enough in the pie for everybody."

**In your opinion, what are the most common mistakes new franchisors or franchisees make?**

For new franchisors, I know from our example and a lot of other people that I've spoken to, when we first start, we're way too eager to please franchisees which means it's not really a win-win situation. It's a win for the franchisees and not so much for the franchisor. It needs to be a win-win for both parties. I think franchising, when done successfully, is such a beautiful system that you can absolutely have a win-win scenario for everybody involved and there aren't many things in life that are genuinely like that.

In terms of new franchisees, it's definitely getting too emotional and overwhelmed but it's that transition of going from employee into first-time business ownership. It's unlike anything else people have ever experienced. I think if you can try and calm down and hold the emotion out of it a little bit, you do much better more quickly.

**What do you believe are the essential qualities and attributes of a successful franchisor or franchise system?**

There has to be enough in the pie for everybody. Like I said before, it's got to be a win-win situation. There are systems I see where I know the franchisor of the company is making a lot of money but there's not enough left in the pie for the franchisee to make a decent income. There needs to be a really delicate balance. If you look at any of the franchising research and see why people go into franchising, the biggest reason is lifestyle and the reason why people exit is lack of profitability.

There needs to be responsibility taken by the franchisee for their profitability as well.

The franchise companies have to make sure that they are set up where there's enough for the company to be able to adequately supply all of the support and the systems that are required and enough for the franchisee to make a good living for the work that they're putting in as well.

"Everyone has different goals in life."

**What advice would you give someone who is thinking about investing in a franchise?**
Everyone has different goals in life. Everyone wants different things and what's right for one person may not be right for another. People need to say, "This is how many hours a week. This is the lifestyle I want to lead, this is how much money I have to invest and this is how much I want in return" then find something that fits that model and that is something that you can also be incredibly passionate about.

**From your perspective, what stops people from being successful?**
Own personal self-doubt.

The main key is people not rising to where they should. People should absolutely be brilliant and let their own light shine, especially in Australia, we have a hard case of tall poppy syndrome. We don't celebrate other people's successes. We are not so happy for people when they do really well and because of that, people minimise themselves and their achievements.

"People should own their brilliance"

They don't think they're good enough to do something in particular. People should own their brilliance and say, "Know what? I can do this and I will be successful," and if you're determined, you can get there.

**What do you believe are the essential qualities or personal attributes of a successful person?**
I think they have a lot of persistence, a lot of resilience. Some advice I received was, "It takes twice as long and costs twice as much to get to where you want to be." You really need to have that staying power. You really need to be committed to your goal, be determined and keep going as long as it takes.

"It takes twice as long and costs twice as much"

**What do you think holds people back from achieving their goal?**
I think sometimes people are so close to that tipping point. Small business statistics in Australia are not brilliant. One in three small businesses fail in the first five years of operation. The first 12 to 24 months of a business is really hard work and a lot of people get a bit too beaten down by that and give up just when they're about to make it.

**How do you describe your management style?**
This has been such a work in progress. I would like to think natural and

authentic. I read a lot of business and leadership books. A lot of them talk about a really autocratic leadership style, which I tried and surprise, surprise, it did not work so well for me. It's taken me a long time to be able to identify what my management style is. I'm pretty laid back, very professional and very down the line. I say what I mean and mean what I say and that works for me.

"I have daily rituals that I perform."

**What are your secrets to be being a successful businesswoman?**

The most important thing is time management. I have two boys. I want to have enough room in my life for my children, for my husband, for my work, for my own health and for my own time. The only way I can be successful on all of those fronts is with really strict time management. My day is broken into 15 minute increments from 6 a.m. down to 10 p.m. and while no day ever runs perfectly, it's very controlled so that I can make sure at the end of the week that I've given adequate time to all of those areas of my life.

**How do you stay focused and on track daily and long-term, especially when the times get tough?**

I have daily rituals that I perform. I wake up in the morning and do yoga, which really starts me off on the right foot for the day so that I can think clearly and make good decisions. Eating well, meditating and exercising so that I can actually stay focused and on track is also important. When we get overwhelmed which, of course, does happen it usually happens to me every two or three months where I'm saying, 'It's all too much' and 'What am I going to do?' You just have to take stock, go for a big walk, take a few deep breaths and put everything back into perspective.

> "I've never been afraid to ask people for help"

Right now, written on my computer screen is, "I keep a helicopter view of life. I think strategically and I focus on the big picture." I have that in front of me all the time so that if I get too bogged down in other people's issues in the day-to-day of things I can remember just to take a step back, fly off in the helicopter and get everything back in perspective.

**Who would you say has inspired you in the past?**
I've been really lucky to have a lot of really brilliant mentors so far in my business journey. I've never been afraid to ask people for help and I allow people to come into my life to share their wisdom and their advice. There are obviously some really wonderful people in the franchising industry who have been amazing. Janine Allis has been someone since the very beginning. Naomi Simpson is not in franchising but she's amazing in the way that she runs her company. And then there's a couple called Matt and Lisa Williams who have personally given me the most help.

> "I've really broken the mould in franchising."

**As a top successful businesswoman, what do you hope to inspire in others?**
I think it's giving it a go. I've really broken the mould in franchising. I didn't start with a partner like a lot of people do. I was in my 20s when I started franchising and I had babies. You don't have to fit the normal mould to do what you want to do. If you've got a dream that's big enough, you can do it.

**What does success mean to you and how does one achieve it or have more of it?**
For me, it's being happy. I have met way too many very financially

successful people that are really unhappy. It's balancing the financial goals that I have with my lifestyle and happiness. I know that we could have grown a lot quicker and a lot sooner had I given up a lot of my family time but it's something that I wanted to maintain always.

I take regular breaks and still make sure that I go on holidays so that I can keep the happiness levels high.

**What is the most important piece of advice anyone has ever given you?**

It's the really simple, work hard and be nice to people.

**What drives you to continue to grow?**

I have no idea. I get asked a lot, "What motivates you? What drives you?" I don't know. I always wanted to achieve a lot. I want to leave my mark on the world. I want to create something amazing that makes a positive impact on other people's lives. I think once you get a taste of achievement, your confidence grows and then it inspires you to achieve even more. I think life is short, you've only got 4,000 weeks on average to live and you've got to make every one count and make it the best that you can be.

**Is there a significant quote or saying that you live your life by?**

Not necessarily, I've got up on my board, "I can and I will, just watch me."

"I can and I will, just watch me."

**What are some of your future plans and goals for the next 5 to 10 years?**

We are aiming to have 100 franchises in operation by 2018. When we get to that stage, we'll see where we want to go from there, whether that's expanding further within Australia or looking internationally it's something that we will have to make a decision on.

For me personally, it's keeping that balance. I have a dream when my children are three and five at school to take a year and continue working at the same time but to go around the world and spend three months in four different countries so that we can see different cultures and learn from them. I can run the business from my laptop while I'm there.

### What is your greatest passion in life?

My family. We made a very drastic change about 18 months ago and we left Sydney. We decided we had had enough of the hectic, chaotic Sydney life and moved to five acres just north of Byron Bay. We've got our absolute sanctuary there. I've got two little boys and watching them grow into the most incredible young men is the greatest honour I could have.

I absolutely love my work but to play and travel around the world with my family is really the most fun I could ever dream up.

### How do you want to be remembered?

Hopefully I'm going to live until I'm 104, that is the plan, otherwise I won't have enough time to fit everything in.

I've still got a long way to go but hopefully it can be as someone who was fun, happy and just made a positive difference in people's individual lives.

*I've never been afraid to ask people for help and I allow people to come into my life to share their wisdom and their advice.*

# CHAPTER 6

## PIPPA HALLAS
Ella Baché

PARIS Ella Baché

# CHAPTER 6

## PIPPA HALLAS -
Ella Baché

*We are constantly working on product innovation.*

Pippa Hallas is the CEO of Ella Baché, a third generation family business and leading skincare company in Australia. Ella Baché distributes its premium skincare products, services and treatments to branded franchise salons, stockists and David Jones stores across the country.

Ella Baché prides itself on sourcing ingredients and manufacturing its products locally. It has a certified education centre, the Ella Baché College of Skin and Beauty Therapy, in North Sydney, which caters for around 100 students on-site each year. It also provides a leading edge online distance learning option to reach aspiring therapists in all parts of Australia.

Pippa is responsible for the strategic direction and daily operations of the business.

## Future Vision

Today, Ella Baché represents 40% of the international skincare market and Pippa believes the company's success is down to its innovative, results driven products and an individual approach to treating the skin.

Ella Baché's enduring educational philosophy and continuous innovation have helped the brand become a global leader in skincare.

Ella Baché's culture of innovation started 60 years ago. Arriving on Australian soil in 1954, Pippa's grandmother, Edith, was quick to notice the lack of skincare available for women and made it her mission to change this.

Pippa is passionate about building on these foundations to help elevate the brand and ensure the company's unique culture remains steadily in place.

"Over the past year, we've done some heavy lifting to ensure that we reignite the passion in our partners, refocus on the company culture and values and reinvest in **brand, education** and **product development** to ensure we're constantly innovating in these key areas. This is the strength of our brand; if our people feel empowered in a healthy culture, real innovation occurs."

Ella Baché's College of Skin and Beauty Therapy enables Ella Baché to strengthen its commitment to education. This reassures our franchise, salon and David Jones distribution outlets of our dedication to excellence, as well as inspiring young therapists to embrace their passion and knowledge about skincare.

Ella Baché currently has 180 salons nationally and future expansion under Pippa's direction will be through new salons supported by a franchise model. This will allow us to support our therapists through extensive marketing, training and education.

**Could you to tell us a little bit about yourself and your company**

Yes, sure. Ella Baché is a leading skincare company in Australia. We had our 60th birthday in Australia last year so I'm actually a third generation C.E.O. It's a family business as well as a franchise business. I have been in the organisation as C.E.O. for about five years and prior to that, head of marketing for about four years and then before that, I had a career in advertising. So that's a little bit about myself.

Looking at Ella Baché, we're a quite diverse business. About 70% - 80%, of our business is made up with our franchising business. We have approximately 170 stores around Australia. We also manufacture here in Sydney and do a lot of the research and development on our products, manufacture them and then distribute them to all of our franchise stores. We also sell through David Jones and run an education program which includes a registered training organisation and an online organisation.

It's quite an unusual and unique business in the sense that it's very much cradle-to-grave or womb-to-tomb in the sense that we are in control of the whole value equation from bringing in mainly young girls into our college, making sure that they work in our stores, etc. and then enabling them to go on to own their own business hopefully in the future.

> "They keep that knowledge for a lifetime."

**Tell us about the company's current position and what the vision for this business is**

Our vision sets us apart in selling in the skincare industry. It is the fact that we believe that knowledge and having great knowledge about your skin basically creates results for your skin and skin health for a lifetime. That really sets the benchmark for us to make sure that we're the leaders in skincare education and knowledge. That then feeds right through our business, right through our franchise system and through the therapists that work in our stores. The customer who walks into our stores learns something about their skin that they haven't learned before and they keep that knowledge for a lifetime which empowers them to have great skin health. So that is essentially the overview of why we exist as a business.

I guess from there, we have a number of strong goals surrounding that. One is to grow the number of franchise stores primarily across Australia at this point. Although we have 170 now, our strategy isn't about volume, it's about putting the right stores in the right positions with the right people and we will achieve our goal this year, which is to open 10 new stores, which is fantastic.

We are also in quite a fast growth position for our college. We launched our high-tech, innovative, online education platform last year, which allows therapists from all over Australia to study in a virtual classroom and become diploma-qualified in beauty therapy, which in turn creates more future salon owners for us.

"We are constantly working on product innovation."

We have also completed a lot of other strategic implementations in the business such as the relaunch of our brand 12 months ago. We have been working on creating new brand imagery, a new store design, new uniforms for all of our therapists and franchisees and new packaging. So it's been a really, really big, exciting project. We are constantly working on product innovation. There's always a lot going on.

**What do you think were some of the factors that contributed to your company's exciting growth?**

I think there are three things. One is reinvesting in the brand and making sure that we are inspirational and relevant not only to our existing customers but also to the next generation. So that's created a lot of interest and noise in the marketplace.

We've got a really fantastic franchise model. Ours is quite unique in the sense that we give our franchisees so much support from marketing to training and business, etc.

"We don't charge any royalties or marketing levies."

In our financial model we don't charge any royalties or marketing levies so we have had a lot of people who are attracted to that, compared to other business models.

**What are some of the most exciting changes you have experienced over the many years?**

For me, on a personal level, I have got a marketing background so I love brand building and reinventing the brand and the marketing side of things. For me, it's the recent one of transforming the brand but also working at changing our digital space. The whole digitisation of the world creates so much change and dynamism that we have to apply to our businesses as business leaders. We need to make sure we pick some really key projects in that space that we can integrate into more traditional marketing elements.

"1% inspiration, 99% perspiration."

It's really exciting. I think just the complexity of how the younger generation behaves and responds to brands and essentially interacts and buys from brands is really exciting.

**Are the younger generation part of your demographic or is it across all ages?**

Yes, it is across all ages. Our customer base is primarily from about 30 upwards and we call these people "Suddenly 30" because that's when the aging process becomes a bit visible on everyone's skin, especially in Australia.

**What do you believe was your biggest sacrifice in getting the business off the ground?**

It's funny that I don't see it as a sacrifice. I love what I do but I think it's certainly hard work and it's, what do they say, 1% inspiration, 99% perspiration. So if you can put that as a sacrifice... but you just have to love what you do, otherwise you just wouldn't do it.

**If there was one key area in management that you would do differently, what would it be?**

I always say managing people and franchisees is your greatest challenge but also your greatest reward. For me, personally, it was becoming more experienced in developing my own skillset in the area of management. I certainly had to learn tough love and I got myself into situations early on where I was probably too kind and became too close to people, which made it hard to drive accountabilities through the business.

"I certainly had to learn tough love."

**What would you say has been the highlight for the business so far?**

Gosh, there are so many. For me, one of my highlights, and this wasn't so much a financial highlight, it's more of a personal highlight, was getting involved with Jessica Watson, the youngest girl who sailed solo around the world.

Working in a business which is predominately female, we certainly believe that backing females and particularly young girls is really important. This was one of the first projects I worked on when I first became C.E.O. The highlight was watching Jess leave her home state in Queensland and have every challenge thrown at her from the media, from the public, etc. and watching her overcome these challenges and literally sail around the world and come back into Sydney Harbour where literally the whole of Australia was watching her and cheering her on. It still actually gives me goose bumps today. It was really amazing.

"You are going to be out of your comfort zone quite a lot but that's okay."

**What tips would you give to other businesswomen who are getting into business?**

I have thought about this over the last couple of weeks because it was International Women's Day recently and I spoke to quite a few school girls. Some of my personal tips were about self-belief and confidence. I think a lot of the time you have to fake it until you make it. You are going to be out of your comfort zone quite a lot but that's okay.

"Follow your instincts"

I also think we need to support other women. I have seen so many women, not in our organisation but other larger corporate organisations, where women are quite hard on each other. I think women probably need to be a bit more supportive of each other in the work place.

"You have to be respected but you don't have to be liked."

Another one would be to follow your instincts and to follow your gut. I think, as women, we've got really strong instincts and sometimes we question that and I know, for myself, the times I have not followed my gut has been when I have got things wrong. It took me a while to have the self-belief to just keep backing myself like that and then the last one would probably have to be...as someone told me earlier on in my career, that you have to be respected but you don't have to be liked. Make sure you constantly gain respect from each other but don't worry about being liked. I think growing up and going from being in your 20s when you're quite social and hanging out to then being in the C.E.O. position, it can be quite lonely. It's all about respect.

"You must have a good network."

**You said sometimes sitting in that C.E.O. position can be a little lonely at times**

Yes, definitely. You must have a good network. I think having really good go-to people, whether it's a formal mentor or a friend or family or just people you can just pick up the phone and have really honest conversations with, is really important.

**When did you first discover that you had entrepreneurial talent?**

I can recall when I was six, seven or even eight, I grew up in a house with lots of fruit trees out the back and we used to sell fruits and lemonade and all sorts of stuff out the front of our driveway quite often, to make some pocket money.

And then the next thing I did when I was in my teens was when I was travelling. I came across this amazing art gallery with lots of pottery and art that had been done by people with Down Syndrome but because it was in the middle of nowhere, they had no customers so I asked them if I could take some of their products to Sydney and set up a store at Paddington Market, which is quite a trendy marketplace in the centre of Sydney in the eastern suburbs. I sold their products for about 12 months and that was really cool. It was great. So I've always had it in me, whether I did it well or not. Who knows?

**What is your approach to marketing and how do you get the Ella Baché name out in the marketplace?**

Yes, you have got to absolutely keep getting out there. I think it's just about understanding your customer and understanding where they use media and how they want to interact with your brand and building a strategy back from that. As I was saying before, there is so much change going on. It's not like 5 or 10 years ago where you probably created a media plan with your media agent and you just stuck to that for 12 months.

I think it's much more complex these days with digital media and the integration between that and other forms of media. For us, it's just a matter of understanding the best way to reach out to our consumers and then putting a mix together between traditional and non-traditional media.

"It's super important that we all work together."

A big part of these days is literally on your phone. Everyone is on their phone and interacting with their phone as soon as they open their eyes in the morning.

Building the inspirational part of our brand still needs to be in fashion magazines and billboards and things like that.

But I guess as a franchise group, it's super important that we all work together, all of our franchisees as well as the franchisors, to make sure we are really aligned and we are taking one message out to the market and executing it completely and with precision on what Ella Baché stands for.

"People have to engage with the brand on an emotional level."

**What are your top tips for effectively branding your business?**

Certainly for a business like this, I think inspiration has to come into it. People have to engage with the brand on an emotional level. The whole world gets so caught up in lead generation and revenue generation, we forget about why people interact with brands in the first place and that's because they aspire to a brand and they want to emotionally connect to one. So that side can't be underestimated.

> "We needed to be really consistent."

Free media and being really innovative and creative with our brand. We're not Coca Cola and we don't have the budget Coca Cola does, so we need to be creative and do things like the Jessica Watson initiative I was talking about before to get the brand out there. We are constantly thinking about PR and digital marketing and different ways that we can build the brand and, in turn, the business.

I'm so used to working in a creative environment where I feel like anyone can spend their way to brand success but to be really creative and innovative and work a budget really, really hard and create leverage is much harder and much more rewarding.

**When was the brand ready to think about franchising?**

It was actually in the late 1990s and we had hundreds of salons across Australia. The Trade Practices Act was very different at that time but it very much forced us to, as a business, formalise our agreements to primarily protect our brand and to drive consistency through the network but also to protect the products that were stocked in our stores and how we conducted the therapy side of the business. We needed to be really consistent.

So those were our motivators and I think we knew that to go to that next stage in the business, we needed to formalise and become a bit more sophisticated about our systems and processes. Subsequently, agreements in franchising was the natural step.

**How did you sell your first franchise? Did they come from within those stores already?**

Yes. So there was a big strategy to convert the stores into franchises, which was what happened and we also opened some company-owned franchise stores, which became the flagship stores for franchising. Later on we sold those to franchisees and they're still within our network today, which is great.

**How did the brand evolve from start-up to now and how you market it?**

It's interesting. I think the brand evolved like society evolved in a way. I look back at a lot of our old marking material, which is so iconic. You just couldn't get away with doing a lot of it today. So as a brand, we've always been quite irreverent and cheeky in our personality but what you got away in the '70s and the '80s, you can't get away with today.

I think I had a reminder of that last year when we launched our new brand campaign. One of the visuals is a shot of four girls who are beautiful, natural-looking girls but you can't see anything that you shouldn't see. There are no boobs or anything like that in there but in one of the images, the girls were smiling and in another they weren't smiling. The image where they weren't smiling was banned by the Outdoor Media Association because it was deemed as too sexual. So I think that was a reminder. When the brand started, we had women who were naked from the chest up facing the camera whereas today you couldn't even see anything and it was still banned. So you've got to be careful of what's going on in society.

And then secondly, as I was saying before, it's how consumers use media and how the internet has totally transformed the way we communicate and market.

"Communicate, communicate, communicate. Franchising at the end of the day is just people with a system around it"

**What has been one of biggest challenges you've had to face in the franchise business and how did you overcome it?**

In the company's history, it was introducing franchising into an old business model. We were the first skincare company to franchise in Australia and we had hundreds of amazing therapists and loyal, passionate clients and business partners who had no idea what franchising meant and were very fearful of it. I think that was probably one of the biggest challenges for us, the initial rollout of the franchise system.

How did we overcome it? Just lots of talking, lots of communication, lots of transparency, lots of honesty and I think that's the only way you can do it. Create a proven model, get it started and then communicate, communicate, communicate. Franchising at the end of the day is just people with a system around it so it's the people who can become the most challenging.

**What is the most important thing you have learned about successful franchising?**

Where franchising works so well for us is when you have complete alignment with the people involved in the franchise business so bringing on the right franchisees in the first place is critical. I think then making sure that the expectations are set really clearly upfront and that it's a partnership. It's not all obviously us supporting them, it's got to go both ways.

I also think that where we really see amazing successes with our franchisees is when a franchisee is completely and naturally aligned to everything we do and takes on every initiative that we do.

"It's a people-led business."

**In your opinion, what are the most common mistakes new franchisors or franchisees make?**

That's a really good question. For our business, it's a people-led business. If you've got the right franchisee, obviously the right franchisor, the right staff and then you start building the business, it works really well. I think if you start to try and do things quickly, you get the wrong team in and you get the wrong franchisee in and it's just never going to work.

"Sometimes you need to say no to things"

Sometimes you need to say no to things and people to make sure you draw total alignment between the franchisees and where you put them, which sites and with which demographics. I have seen people grow way too quickly and not be able to sustain their growth.

**What do you believe are the essential qualities and attributes of a successful franchisor or the franchise systems?**

With a franchise system, all the obvious things have to be really watertight like a proven business model and the fact that you can actually make money out of it, the fact that it's relevant to consumers, etc. But I also think that there are soft qualities and attributes, which people often underestimate, and that's making sure that you've got the right culture and the right values in the system and that those values are understood and aligned throughout the network.

"If the people or the culture isn't right, then you're never going to realise the full potential."

So again, we're in the business of people and we have got a system to support them but if the people or the culture isn't right, then you're never going to realise the full potential.

**What advice would you give to someone who is thinking about investing in a franchise?**

I would ask, "Do you have the passion for the industry? Are your key drivers aligned to the key drivers of the franchise system and the business?"

I think money and the financial freedom follows from being passionate and self-driven and in alignment. I would also ask someone who is thinking about investing in franchising if it is something that turns them on and makes them feel excited and passionate.

**From your perspective, what stops people from being successful?**

Self-belief, confidence, drive, perseverance and commitment.

"You have to have a vision. "

**What do you believe are the essential qualities or personal attributes of a successful person?**

You have to have a vision. You have to know where you're going. You have to be able to, quite often, tell that story and that vision and communicate that to other people if you want them to follow. You can't tell people what to do. You have to engage people and bring them on the journey. You have to believe in yourself. You have to be passionate about what you do. You have to love what you do. You have to be willing to work hard and put in the time to really get there.

"You have to engage people and bring them on the journey."

**What do you think holds people back from achieving their own goals?**
Lack of focus, lack of drive, lack of confidence and lack of understanding what their goals are.

**How would you describe your own management style?**
My management style - I'm pretty collaborative. I'm really open. I love working with people. I'm not someone who enjoys sitting in an office with the door shut by myself. I'm very intuitive but at the same time, I do need some evidence-based science about decision making, although I can move really, really quickly but I think on the flip side of that, I just have to make sure that I slow down to bring people along for the journey and I don't move too quickly.

"No one can do it by themselves."

**What are your secrets to being a successful businesswoman?**
I think it's working with other people, especially other women, and supporting each other. It's being able to relate to people and get the best out of people. It's being able to put out my hand or pick up the phone if I need help. I certainly don't know the answers to everything and I certainly know that I need people around me to make me successful.

It tends to take time to build up a fabulous team of people who can play to your strengths and be better than you in so many other areas and I think that's critical. No one can do it by themselves.

> "Chunk it all down and understand what your priorities are"

**How do you stay focused and on track on a daily basis or long-term, especially when the times get tough?**

Sometimes when times are tough and you can get really overwhelmed, I think it's just having the ability to chunk everything down and work out what needs to happen next and what's the most critical thing that has to be done next. And then one thing leads to another.

If you can't chunk it all down and understand what your priorities are, that's when it can completely overwhelm you and paralyse you or you end up doing the wrong things first and never getting anywhere.

**Who would you say has inspired you in the past?**

I think the typical one that always comes to mind is Richard Branson and people like that. You look at some people, such as him, who have done the most incredible and innovative things that are just on another level. I think it is so amazing to have that vision. For example, sending someone into space and being able to absolutely transform an industry. I admire people who think so big.

> "It's okay to go against the grain but you have to be bold and you have to be brave."

I was reading an article yesterday that Bob Geldof wrote. His philosophy is - it's okay to go against the grain but you have to be bold and you have to be brave. Those are the types of people who really inspire me.

"Everyone has potential."

I hope to bring out the best in people. Everyone has potential. As a leader, I hope to bring out everyone's potential to be the best person they can be in the workplace.

Of course you can talk about financial success but I think it's about being turned on with what you do, being satisfied, feeling like you're progressing, achieving, being creative and at the end of the day, being happy.

**What is the most important piece of advice anyone has ever given you?**

I think what I mentioned earlier, "You don't have to be liked but you have to be respected," probably rings true for me as a C.E.O.

Follow your instincts.

"Don't do things better than people. Do it differently."

I think for me, I've got the luxury of working in a family business. My father owns a business and he hasn't worked in the business day after day for about 20 years. My dad is an entrepreneur and he's really, really creative so he's always taught me, "Don't do things better than people. Do it differently. If you do things differently, you create your own pathway. Competitors can't follow you if you do things differently." That's always been a match, so that very much stuck with me.

> "We have always got a really fantastic and exciting strategic plan"

**What drives you to continue to grow?**

I just love what I do. I just love progression. I love being able to see things come to fruition. Not everything works but it's the process and the creativity and working with other people and growing a fabulous brand. Especially in this organisation, I get to watch lots of young girls come out of our college and see them growing into amazing businesswomen in their own right. That keeps me going.

**What are some of your personal or business plans and goals for the next 5 to 10 years?**

On a personal level, I'm about to have my second child in two months so that's kind of exciting. It'll be an interesting time. I will have a toddler who is two-and-half and a young baby.

On a business level, we've got pretty exciting and ambitious growth plans. It's growing the franchise business and it's growing our educational side of the business so we will continually take the business and make it more relevant and we want to get Ella Baché into more and more people's lives.

We have always got a really fantastic and exciting strategic plan that we work from annually as well as a five-year prospective but to say Ella Baché is really an inspirational brand for the consumers and it's also a business that people to want to be part of, is certainly my overarching plan.

**What is your greatest passion in life?**

I think certainly being a mum. I think being a mum to young kids is amazing but I also love being a C.E.O. and working with people. And again going back to what I love doing, which is working and building a fabulous brand as well as working with and watching some amazing people grow throughout their careers.

I feel lucky as a woman that I can manage to do both. It's not always easy but I can manage to do both. They give me a lot of satisfaction, both of them.

**How do you want to be remembered?**

I think I'd love to be remembered for being an amazing mum and a loving mother as well as an amazing and inspiring female C.E.O.

*I love what I do but I think it's certainly hard work. It's 1% inspiration, 99% perspiration.*

# CHAPTER 7

## CHRIS TAYLOR

Aussie Pooch Mobile

# CHAPTER 7

## CHRIS TAYLOR -
Aussie Pooch Mobile

*Stay focused on your goals and don't give up.*

Christine Taylor is the managing director and founder of Aussie Pooch Mobile. Her career began when she started an innovative dog clipping and grooming service in 1985, when she was just 16 years of age. A few years later, Chris expanded this service to include mobile dog washing units travelling directly to customer's homes. The company was launched as a single mobile dog wash unit in 1990 and as demand increased, the business rapidly grew.

After some experimentation, a huge amount of courage, a feasibility study and the full support of her husband, Chris created and launched the Aussie Pooch Mobile Dog Wash and Grooming Franchise in 1991. This is where her journey within the franchise industry began.

The Aussie Pooch Mobile was the first franchise system of its kind and is the premier dog wash and care company in the world!

Dogs are lining up for our service!

The company also operates under the name, 'The Pooch Mobile' with master franchisees in United Kingdom, Malaysia, New Zealand, New Caledonia and the USA. There are now almost 200 franchisees across the world.

Chris says, "Being in a position to help others become successful in a field they are passionate about, is very rewarding." Chris has created a culture of 'We Care' within Aussie Pooch Mobile. With the help of an experienced and loyal support team, each franchisee is provided with guidance and support to help them achieve their goals.

Chris has been awarded many accolades over the years due to the success of Aussie Pooch Mobile including, 1994 Young Achiever of The Year, 1996 Qld Telstra Business Woman of the Year, 2005 Australian Woman in Franchising and in 2012 she was accepted into the Franchising Hall of Fame. The individual franchisees have also won many awards for their business success. In 2013, Chris, her husband David and Aussie Pooch Mobile as a whole were recognised with the inaugural National Variety Chairman's award for their efforts in fundraising for Variety the children's charity.

Franchising with Aussie Pooch Mobile allows other dog lovers to be rewarded for their efforts. They will have the good fortune of building a successful business while doing something they enjoy.

**Could you tell us a little bit about yourself and your company?** I run Aussie Pooch Mobile, a mobile dog washing company. I grew up in a bait and tackle shop, so I came from a self-employed background. I worked in a telephone answering service, setting up appointments for different insurance groups. I also had my own telephone answering service before the days of mobile phones and paging services that was personalised. I ran a business called "Our Other Office" and I answered people's phones for them and acted as their secretary.

Then along came the grooming salon. We bought our own property at 18 and ran our grooming salon from there. We got married and expanded onto another property which had dog kennels on it. So I started breeding dogs, had dog kennels, had the grooming salon, had a whole heap of things going along and was always looking for that next opportunity. I realised very quickly that my clients that had their dogs hair cut also had other dogs at home that didn't necessarily need a haircut but they smelled and they needed their ears cleaned and brushed and groomed and a good wash and nails clipped and all that sort of thing so I started going by hand, with the little dogs tied to the clothes line, with a bucket and sponge. And I was washing in between my grooming haircuts.

From there, I was like, 'This is crazy! I'm getting such a big demand for washing. What about all the dogs that are just in people's back yards who don't actually have a dog that needs a haircut? How do I reach them?' So I started marketing towards that and I very quickly had a full diary, a couple of days a week. And I was like, 'Well this is crazy! How do I expand it from there?' So I went on a belated honeymoon but didn't have a lot of things to do there so the whole time I was ringing back home to a young lady who was working for me and going, "Find this out, find that out."

A week later I confessed to my husband, David and said, "This is what I've been doing and this is what we're going to do. We're going to have little trailers running around, we're going to have a mobile dog washing service." And he was like, "Yep?" And I'm like "Yep, so this is what we are going to do. We're going to have six." But then David says, "No! We are only having one and we're testing it." After a bit of arguing I said, "Fine, we'll have one and we'll test it and I'll prove you wrong." So then I rang my father and he put our first trailer together. So within two weeks of coming home, I was out on the road with the Aussie Pooch Mobile.

**Tell us about the company's current position, how things are tracking and what the vision for the business is**

People love their pets, in particular, dogs. With one in three households in the western world having a dog, there's plenty of room for growth. Pet owners are humanising their dogs and becoming pet parents and research shows that pet parents are spending more on their pets.

We have currently got 175 units on the road and we are washing in excess of 20,000 dogs per month in Australia alone but we're also in the UK and the US. We're also expanding our range of products which are available to our customers and we're building our own brand with our own labels.

**Can you describe your reaction to being the recipient of some amazing awards like Franchise Woman of the Year, Telstra Business Woman for Queensland and Young Achiever of the Year and also being recognised in the Franchise Council of Australia's Hall of Fame?**

The reaction is awesome. The awards themselves allow you an opportunity to reflect and to actually look at what you have actually achieved. It's something I do recommend every business owner does and we do it within our company just as a reflection every year of what have we achieved. It's so easy to focus on the negative but the reflection allows you to actually reward yourself. It's absolutely awesome to be recognised by industry leaders and your peers for all your hard work. I've found that the awards have provided me with a platform to reach out and help others.

"A reflection every year of what have we achieved. It's so easy to focus on the negative but the reflection allows you to actually reward yourself. "

**What do you think are some of the factors that contributed to your company's exciting growth?**

I think it was being in the right place at the right time and making sure I looked for opportunities and took them.

The opportunity to share my passion for the care of dogs and the people who share in my business, to ensure that they also run profitable businesses, is paramount.

"I looked for opportunities and took them."

When I commenced, it was a time when women were just finding their way in the workforce and franchising was a fairly new concept. So when a 21-year-old young lady started a new concept of travelling to people's homes to wash and care for their dog, then expanded through franchising, the people in the media loved it. I quickly learned to take advantage of that and use every situation to maximise this opportunity.

> "The whole room laughed."

I think passion, belief in myself, never losing sight of the end goal, sharing with others, creating a great team, staying humble, working hard and ensuring you give back to your team and your community wherever possible is what contributed.

**What are some of the most exciting changes you've experienced?**

I think how people view the business and those within it. What was basically a non-existent business and concept has become part of everyday life for dog owners.

One of the stories that I have is when I won the Telstra Business Woman of the Year Award, we were in a room of 400 or 500 leading business owners. We were walking in and were like, "Oh my god! Look at this room of leaders!" And we sat at the table and they announced the finalists. When it came to announcing Chris Taylor from Aussie Pooch, which is a dog washing business, the whole room laughed.

I put my shoulders back, and I thought to myself, you will be laughing on the other side because, I tell you, that laugh just motivated me so much more. Win or not, I know that this is successful and you guys will be proven wrong. When they announced me as the winner you could not have dropped a pin on the ground and not heard it. It was just amazing for me to prove them wrong.

We went from creating our own brand product to launching our aroma care products and doggie facials, to combat the use of water when there was a drought in Australia.

> "Not everything can happen today."

**What do you think was your biggest sacrifice in getting your business off the ground?**
I don't know whether you can call anything a sacrifice when you absolutely believe in something. You just do what needs to be done to make things happen without questioning. And when you believe, and you're passionate about it, others just come along for the ride.

**If there was one key area in management that you would do differently, what would it be?**
It's easy to say if I'd known then what I know now but the fact is you don't know at the time. I would have had systems in place to allow people to take the next step within our business to growth further.

When you're in the midst of a growing, thriving business and people are saying you've got to find balance and you're like, "You tell me how to find balance, that's ridiculous! Absolutely ridiculous! I've got this to do, that to do. How can I find balance?" And then they say you need an exit strategy. "Exit strategy? I'm trying to grow this thing; I don't want to think about exit strategy!" But when I look back, I can now show you how I've found balance and I'm now working on my exit strategy. So it's really paramount to take that on board but I think that it's important to understand that not everything can happen today.

**What would you say has been the highlight for your business so far?**
I think the people within it, we have an absolutely awesome team, and being at the forefront of creating an industry, becoming a household name and providing a service that people rely on to care for their pets.

"Stay focused on your goals"

Whether it be the customers and their pets, or our operators, or the team around us, our family, or the people that support us on a personal level. Sometimes we think we created the business so we can make friends.

**What tips would you give to other businesswomen who are getting into business?**

I'd say believe in yourself, research, set goals, work hard and keep some balance in your personal and business life. Take those mini-breaks. Stay focused on your goals and don't give up. Also, don't give up on even the smallest project too soon. I see so many business people and they say, "That didn't work." And I'm looking at their business idea and I'm thinking, "You just gave up too soon."

"Don't think that you have to do it all yourself."

Ask for help and be prepared to give help too. Don't think that you have to do it all yourself.

**So when did you first discover that you had entrepreneurial talent?**

I think I never stopped to think I had entrepreneurial talent. I just got on with doing what needed to be done to ensure that my ideas grew and prospered. This is how I still operate. In thinking about it though, I suppose that I was born into entrepreneurship with the examples I was set by my family and my background.

"I call entrepreneurship 'thinking stupid"

I call entrepreneurship 'thinking stupid' because nobody would've thought that anyone could've started a business of washing dogs. That was 'stupid' so when I come up with a new idea I say, "Come on, think 'stupid.' I want to think of the most stupid idea ever. It's amazing what's come of that e.g. the amount of publicity we created simply because we started doing doggie facials. It's really about not limiting yourself to what's already out there. Take the bull by the horns and run with the craziest idea ever.

"Think small to grow big."

**What is your approach to marketing and how did you get your name out in the marketplace?**

When we first began, there was absolutely no budget for marketing. I didn't even know what a budget was. I had no money so I just did whatever I could that didn't cost any money or that I could easily measure the results of.

The other thing that we do is think small to grow big. We look back to what we did that generated the business when we first began. It was the networking, it was the feet on the ground, it was seeing the person with the dog and dropping a leaflet in their mailbox and telling them what we actually did. It wasn't about putting a full page advert in the paper. If we did do any advertising we looked at the results of that 50 dollars we spent and wondered how we could make that bigger and better the next time.

Aussie Pooch Mobile looks after the national marketing side of things. We set up their website, we manage the national Facebook page as well as the creation of pamphlets but the branding of the business is what the head office looks after. The smaller things are what we train the franchisee to do. It's not about how much money you spend, it's about what you do with the results.

"Involve yourself in your community."

**What are your top tips for effectively branding a business?**

Be consistent in everything that you do with your marketing material, your cards, your flyers, your website and your Facebook pages. You need to turn up on time, provide exceptional customer service and everything that goes along with it and you need to be memorable.

I think you also need to involve yourself in your community.

**When did you know that it was time to think about franchising your brand?**

I had 6 operators on the road and we were looking at whether we employed them or whether we put them on a contract basis. When I became pregnant with our first daughter, I couldn't go out on the road. I couldn't wash the dogs that I had before. It grounded me but it also gave me the opportunity to do the research that I needed to work out how I was going to keep up with the demand and what I needed to do to expand further.

I needed a way to expand that saw people taking on more than a job and that embedded them into their customers' lives, of being the go-to person to care for their customers' dogs. I didn't want anybody to see themselves as just a dog washer. I needed people who believed in my passion and took ownership of everything that they did. Franchising came up as the way to expand. Back then, franchising was pretty new, so there weren't a lot of people that you could go to. But now, it's awesome. The franchising industry is great. You have people that share their ideas and it's just grown and we've grown along with it.

> "Providing an exceptional service at an affordable price is paramount to anyone's success."

**How did you promote and sell your first franchise then?**

All of this was done through word of mouth and company owned conversions and these strategies are still used today. We have company owned sites, we put people in to work them, then we help them build their business and they then convert into franchisees. We also have word of mouth where people hear about us through customers and people who know people.

**How has the brand evolved from start up until now?**

I suppose it's essential to know that the traditional methods of marketing are still there. Providing an exceptional service at an affordable price is paramount to anyone's success. I believe embedding your business in your local community is essential.

Now we have a lot more flexibility in marketing but more importantly, we have ways to measure the results.

With the internet and social media and all these opportunities, there are so many ways that you can build your brand simply by changing a few words and then measuring the results.

> "It is important that you're choosy."

**What was your international expansion strategy?**

Expansion is really about the right people finding you. So doing your research and making people aware of your intentions and then welcoming them to your doors. It is important that you're choosy. Taking on another country brings loads of challenges so it's paramount that you have the systems and the people in place in your home country that can support the established business while you go off and do the expansion because obviously the best person to expand is someone who knows the business inside out. It has to be the founder or someone who's been with them a long time.

> "When we first began there were loads of doubters."

**What has been one of the biggest challenges you've had to face in the franchise business and how did you overcome it?**

When we first began there were loads of doubters. "That's a nice idea for a young girl," but along the way I had people who believed in me and one of those guys was our solutions supplier. I needed a solution that we could wash the dogs with. I wanted to get our own brand label but the big guys didn't want to know about me and they were just like, "Oh, that's a nice idea. Why would I put our product and our brand on your label?" And I was trying to convince them and telling them my expansion ideas and they're just like, "Yeah, well you've done alright for now but, you know. Nice idea for a young girl." Our solutions supplier, that we still use to this day, said, "That is a nice idea for a young girl; I like the way you think. I'm 65 years old, I moved from New Zealand, I'm retired and I don't need to work but this is an awesome industry and I reckon we can do something together." And he believed in me. He was one of my strongest supporters.

**What is the most important thing you have learned about successful franchising?**

Your people. You have to invest in them and help them believe in themselves and their own abilities and help them grow. People invest in you. You have a huge responsibility as a franchisor to hold that responsibility dearly and very much deliver on what you say you're going to do.

As new franchisors we go out selling our first franchise and we're telling people this is what we are going to do. When you do get that first franchisee, it's almost like "Holy cow! I now have to do what I said I was going to do and there's no backing out."

"You can't expect people to know."

You have all of these people that you shared your vision with saying, "Wow! Congratulations! You've got your first franchisee!" and you're sitting there shaking in your boots going, "Oh my God, I am so responsible."

**In your opinion, what are the most common mistakes new franchisors and franchisees make?**

With franchisors, its communication. You can't expect people to know. You can't just assume that others will trust you and know what you're doing so we're very open in the way that we communicate with our franchisees.

With franchisees, I'd say it's communication as well. They need to come to us and tell us what's going on with their lives, be it a sick mum or a car that's just broken down or a family issue. We can't help somebody if we don't know what's happening in their lives.

"You have to share your vision"

**What do you believe are the essential qualities and attributes of the successful franchise or franchise system?**

Your people, your communication, your systems and you have to share your vision. Your culture is also very important.

**What advice would you give to someone who is thinking about investing in a franchise?**

I'd tell them that franchising is a fantastic way to be trained in a new field with support and guidance. I'd tell them to find something that they love, set some business and life goals and share these. They need to do some research, be prepared to work hard and stay focused on their goals and remember to reward themselves for all these little goals.

"Reward themselves for all the little goals."

**What stops people from being successful, from your perspective?**
Giving up too soon! I think that sometimes people aren't successful because they don't take time out to reward themselves. That's the reflection we talked about earlier. And again, you need to find that balance of life and business so you can enjoy all that it has to offer and not lose things along the way.

**What do you believe are the essential qualities or personal attributes of a successful person then?**
They've got to have belief in themselves and their own ability. They need to have a positive attitude and be prepared to help others.

**What do you think holds people back from achieving their goals?**
Not setting them to begin with!

It was the year of our 21st birthday and I said, "This year I'm getting on national TV. I don't care what we do; I don't care how we do it but we will be on national TV." We had birthday parties, we launched the doggie facial and we had all this stuff going on. We had media coverage; it was awesome. It was the 31st of November but we still hadn't been on national TV. We were contacted by the Channel Ten news crew and they said, "Oh, we really like this idea of a dog birthday party. Can we do a doggie Christmas party?" and we said, "Absolutely!" It was a feel good story, so I organised for the TV crew to come out. We had a customer who organised the party for us and we had 10 dogs there. We had the Aussie Pooch van giving the dogs a bath, ready for Christmas Day. Channel Ten filmed it, they had it edited and then something happened, like a cyclone or something and the feel good story got dumped. It's now the 20th December and "there's nothing! How are we going to do this?" 'The Project' program happened to do a story on what's in the news and they picked up on the doggie facial and ran the story on the program.

"I'm not afraid to have the hard conversations."

"We did it!" So don't give up too soon and focus on what you want to achieve. And if it hadn't happened that year, I can tell you I would have absolutely focused on doing everything we possibly could to achieve that goal the very next year.

**So how would you describe your management style?**
Being open and honest and leading by example and I'm not afraid to have the hard conversations.

**What are your secrets to being a successful businesswoman?**
I don't know whether being a successful businesswoman is very different from being successful in business. I would have been successful whether I was male or female or anything in between. Does being a woman have an advantage? In my eyes, and in this business, absolutely! Because I was able to capitalise on it. They didn't expect a 21-year-old girl to be able to do this.

**How do you stay focused and on track, daily and long term, especially when times do get tough?**
Keep a calendar and keep organised. David and I share a calendar and we laugh and tell our friends, whoever puts their appointment in the calendar first, wins. I'll say, "I won that weekend; you've got to do what I want," and he'll say to me, "But that's not in the calendar!" and I'm like, "Yes it is!" and I quickly go and look and realise I forgot to write it, so I'll quickly put it in there.

"Everyone has something to offer."

**Who would you say has inspired you in the past?**
My parents and family and those people who struggle in everyday life, whether it's with personal injury or special children, and what they have overcome. I love people's stories as they show me that everyone has something to offer and you should be thankful for what you have.

**As a top successful businesswoman, what do you hope to inspire in others?**
Find something that you're passionate about and set some goals and then you will have the ability to create balance in your life. You can have it all.

**What does success mean to you then and how does one achieve it or get more of it?**
Success is not a destination but rather a journey. I don't think you can ever say that you're successful without adding what you're successful in. You need to embrace the journey and achieve success in whatever takes your passion.

"You can have it all."

**What is the most important piece of advice anyone has ever given you?**
I'm not sure that the words have always been put into place but the examples I've been set by family and friends have held me in good stead for what life brings my way.

Care, compassion, focus, hard work, believe in yourself are all values that have been embedded within me by my parents, friends and family.

You can have it all.

"You never know how far you can fly until you spread your wings."

**What drives you to continue to grow?**
The people. They believe in me and they rely on me. It's a huge responsibility and one that I embrace.

**Is there a significant quote or saying which you live your life by?**
'You never know how far you can fly until you spread your wings.' My husband, David, bought me this framed picture of an eagle with these words on it when I was questioning where we were heading and how far we should go. He said to me, "You know what your problem is?" I said, "Obviously you're going to tell me" and he said, "You don't have any immediate goals. It's like you've arrived and you don't know where you're heading. You've got all this opportunity but you need to set yourself some goals." I took that on board and about a week later I had this huge framed photo in my office.

**What are some of your future plans and goals, both personally and in business, for the next 5 to 10 years?**
Business continues to grow and we do have a strategy being put into place now to bring on further team members to help us expand further. It will allow us to focus more on growth in dog numbers and expand our product range and services.

Personally, life is changing as our children grow up and leave home and it enables David and I to take advantage of these changes and take some time out to explore other areas of our life and look at where we're heading and how we're going to enjoy our time together.

**What is your greatest passion in life?**
Helping others achieve their goals.

**How do you want to be remembered?**

I believe that if you go to your grave with people remembering you for being a caring, compassionate person and feeling that their world was a better place for you being in it, you've achieved an awesome light in your life. And that's how I'd like to be remembered.

*Providing an exceptional service at an affordable price is paramount to anyone's success.*

# CHAPTER 8

## FRANCESCA WEBSTER

Brazilian Beauty

# CHAPTER 8

**FRANCESCA WEBSTER -**
Brazilian Beauty

*Many business owners actually forget to educate themselves or don't take on a mentor or don't take external advice and guidance.*

Since founding Brazilian Beauty, Francesca has learnt how to succeed in several new highly competitive industries; the beauty industry, the franchise sector and in digital marketing.

Francesca Webster has built her beauty business with the idea of nurturing successful women. In 2004 she began Brazilian Beauty because she wanted to use her corporate skills and strong drive to give others the opportunity to succeed as businesswomen in their own right.

Francesca believes and promotes the brand vision 'the client is king' coupled with the belief that team members receive the same level of fostering as clients. As process and innovation driven by Francesca propel the business forward and improve both the franchisee and client offering, the brand continues to flourish and grow even as it did during the recent tough economic downturn.

Brazilian Beauty, winners of the Lord Mayors Business Award for Small Business Growth in 2014, is headquartered in Queensland. Sixteenth in BRW's Fast Franchise list in 2011, QLD Woman in Franchising 2011, Ernst & Young Entrepreneur Finalist 2012, Brisbane Business News Young Entrepreneur Finalist 2012 and recently Telstra Business Women's Award Finalist 2014, the brand is no stranger to success. Now with 20 locations and a turnover of more than $12 million, Brazilian Beauty has further expansion plans beginning with 6 new salons openings in 2015 and further growth of the Australian Skin Institute brand is also planned for the year.

Francesca's motto is to stay focused on process, be passionate about adding value to the customer experience and don't let anyone tell you that it can't be done.

**Tell us a little bit about yourself and your company?**
I'm from the UK originally and I grew up in Chester, which is in northwest England. It is a small, beautiful Roman city and a gorgeous place to live. I was a pretty badly behaved teenager and I actually left school when I was 16.

I managed to get a great little job working for Shell UK Limited as a receptionist. That would have been over 25 years ago now. I'm 42, so I got my first job when I was 16. Prior to that, I did have a job working in a clothing store when I was 14 and I absolutely loved that.

Around that time, I was working in reception but computers were really not used in the workplace; they were just being introduced at Shell. Nobody really knew how to use one and few had seen one before. I was fortunate as we had a computer at home. I suppose because I was young, I picked things up quite quickly in our location in Stanlow, where five and a half thousand people work. I was 'identified' as somebody who could use as a computer so Shell decided to send me on some courses

Before I knew it, I kind of started this career in IT which did start off slowly. I then moved to London with Shell when I was 18 and it is where I met my partner, from whom I'm now divorced. By the age of 21, I had two children which, when I think back on it, is crazy. My children are now 21 and 22 years old. They'll often say to me, "Oh, my God, Mum, I can't believe that by the time you were our age you had two children!"

But I went straight back to work for Shell. Then I went to work for Morgan Stanley and later for the BBC in the IT department. I was initially a Microsoft-certified trainer, then a Microsoft-certified network engineer. I then did a Cisco Networks course over in the U.S. and also Nortel Networks. I did everything, from desktop design and implementation to network architecture. I had a great time. I was a contractor in most of my roles and earned lots of money.

In the year 2000, I moved to Australia. My ex-husband was Australian so I moved to Australia with him and we broke up shortly after that. I thought, "Do I go back to the UK or do I stay in Australia?" In Australia at that time, the IT contractors' wages weren't particularly high but I had some money in a house. I thought, "There's never been a better time to go out and try something new and start my own business."

I think, in my life, I've always been surrounded by people who have owned their own businesses. Prior to that, I just never felt the need to open my own business because things were flying along really nicely in IT.

When I broke up with my husband, I was in a situation where I needed to earn money but I also wanted to spend time with my children. The IT industry was great but it relied on me being there for every hour of every day that I was paid for.

I looked around at lots of different industries and thought, "What would I love? What do I think I'd be good at?" I suppose with my kind of system processing and reporting background, I was looking for an industry in which I could use that corporate skill set and apply it to a business to produce a better result. Produce a better result for the clients and the clients' experience and also to produce a better result for the team members and their personal development in that industry.

My business opened in May 2004 and it grew from there.

## Tell us about your company's current position, how things are tracking and what the vision for the business is

The company's current position is great and we currently have 20 Brazilian Beauty locations. We also have vertical integration throughout our company. I trademarked another brand called the Australian Skin Institute which produces skincare products and also other consumer retail products that are sold within the 20 locations. This year, I plan to sell the skincare range, the Australian Skin Institute skincare range, outside of the Brazilian Beauty brand. We will be looking for international distribution channels for our products.

> "We constantly reassess the business."

I'm going to continue to grow the franchise side. We're hoping to hit 50 locations in less than four years, which I think is achievable.

**What factors do you think have contributed to your company's exciting growth so far?**

Initially choosing a service and being able to fill a 'pain point' for consumers. Consumers were looking for a professional service that had great client experience and great customer follow up.

I think positioning the right people in the right roles; without a doubt, the systems, the processes and the procedures. I think always looking at the business from the client's perspective. We can't be doing what we were doing eight years ago just because it worked eight years ago. I think the fact that we constantly reassess the business.

Communication in our organisation at every level and having those clear lines of communication, regular meetings and regular feedback, whether that's from the customer, our therapists, our coordinators, our franchisees or head office team member.

**What are the most exciting changes you've experienced?**

In the early days when we opened three salons in 18 months. We literally had customers saying, "I'm so glad that you're doing this. I'm so glad that you're open."

> "You just have to do whatever's required."

The introduction of technology in the beauty industry which, from a client's perspective, would be IPL hair removal, LED skin treatments and IPL treatments.

**What do you believe was your biggest sacrifice in getting the business off the ground?**

Definitely my time and it still is to a certain degree. When you own your own business, it's definitely not a 9 to 5 job. You just have to do whatever's required.

Sometimes you can't go to that event or wedding or your child's sports day but fortunately, I really love what I do.

**If there was one key area in management that you would do differently, what would it be?**

I think if there's one key area that I would do differently, it would have been to get help earlier, to work on me.

Many business owners actually forget to educate themselves or don't take on a mentor or don't take external advice and guidance. If your leadership is right, that will filter down throughout the whole organisation.

> "Many business owners actually forget to educate themselves."

**What would you say has been the highlight for your business so far?**

Having franchisees, female franchisees, who join the brand but who have never owned their own business before, take on a Brazilian Beauty franchise and end up earning more money than their professional husband. That's definitely a highlight.

"Find a mentor who's been successful."

Some business highlights would be being awarded the FCA Franchise Woman of the Year for Queensland, being an EY finalist, a Telstra Business Woman finalist and winning the Brisbane Lord Mayor's Small Business Award.

Another highlight is definitely when I held a lecture on marketing for third-year business students at QUT last year. I was totally excited because I was like, "Oh, my God. I never went to uni. Guys, this is my first day at uni. How exciting!" They all clapped.

**What tips would you give to other businesswomen who are getting into business?**

I'd say research your industry. Find a mentor who's been successful. Research similar industries on the internet. Look at those trials and tribulations. Look at the downfalls and pitfalls that other people have had and have learned from.

**When did you first discover that you had entrepreneurial talent?**

When I set up Brazilian Beauty I realised that I could influence change. I had a sense of what consumers wanted. I could get my head around how to manage people. I would have been 31, I think, at the time so I was definitely a late bloomer.

With Brazilian Beauty, the way I feel about it and the way I feel about business now, is that it just fits me. It fits me like a glove. I don't find anything challenging about it. I feel like I instinctively know what to do in my business or how to fix it when things are going off-track a little bit.

"I instinctively know what to do in my business"

**What is your approach to marketing and how did you get your name and your business name out into the marketplace?**

Initially, we opened the doors to the first store and I suppose, like any small business owner, we thought, "Here we go. The people are just going to walk in through the door. Clients are going to walk in, this is going to be great." After two or three days we realised that that wasn't the case. So we just went hard. We were a 'disruptive innovator' at that time. We went hard just to generate sales and get people through the door.

We strategically chose the name Brazilian Beauty because at that time, the Brazilian wax was pretty taboo in the market. So whether they loved it or hated it, we had people talking about it from day one. At that time, I didn't even know what PR was but we generated an awful lot of free PR because of the name.

"We were a 'disruptive innovator"

As the brand's grown we now find ourselves in 2015 in a very competitive marketplace yet again, where we're going to have to bring out some of that disruptive innovation.

"Choose a great name"

Having a background in technology, I absolutely adore the digital arena. I love it. I actually have two full time team members, just working on our digital marketing and social media. It's so measurable. It's so targeted and you have the ability to segment data.

**What are your top tips for effectively branding a business?**

I think it's to choose a great name, initially.

Have a clear idea of who your target customer is. Talk to those customers. I think consistency in your branding and your approach. The way that you look, your message, your frequency and your content.

**When did you know it was time to think about franchising the brand?**

The initial business objective when we opened was to open multiple stores, so we opened three company-owned stores.

One of our main objectives, initially, was "Hey, I really want to create this business where I don't need to be there all the time." It's got the systems, the processes, the reporting, the consistency throughout so that I didn't need to be there and I achieved that with the three company-owned stores.

Then I literally had people knocking on the door saying "I want to buy a franchise." I weighed up the options of "Do we grow via a company-owned model or via a franchise model?" The restriction with a company-owned model was access to capital of about $350,000.

I decided to go with the franchise model. I truly believe that the nurturing and individual touch a franchisee can put on their business and the way they can drive it just by them being there has a massive influence on the performance of the salon.

When I talk about the franchisees being there, the majority of our franchisees do not work in their businesses, they work on them. So it's about team member management, rather than physically being in there serving customers.

**When did you start to promote and sell franchises?**
To be honest, not until three years ago. Prior to that, the business grew organically. We put a few franchise ads out over the years and we did a couple of expos. Apart from the expos and a little bit of advertising . . . the growth was organic, people were customers, they'd seen the brand and they thought, "Well, this is a great little business model," so they approached us in that way.

Three years ago I asked the question, "I've got a really nice little business. It's doing really well. I love it and it's easy to manage but do I want to keep it here or do I want to take it to the next level?" The conscious decision was to grow, so the past three years have been a question of, how do we surround ourselves with the right people for future growth? What vertical integration can we make happen that's good for the franchisor and brilliant for the franchisee? What do we need to look like as an organisation in order to facilitate 50 stores? What do we need to like operationally? What does our marketing need to look like? What does our support need to look like?

"We love a bit of change here!"

**How did the brand evolve from start up until now in how you market?**

We love a bit of change here! When we opened the doors to Brazilian Beauty in 2004, we did Brazilian waxing and spray tanning and that was it. Now, we've got a full range of products with advanced skin treatments.

We're constantly listening to our customers and we deliver what they want. We never implement a treatment because we think, "Oh, I really like that. I think we'll get that in." We always do the market research first, always research through our customers.

We've evolved so much, from doing two treatments to now doing a suite of over 100 treatments.

**What has been one of the biggest challenges you've had to face in the franchise business and how did you overcome it?**

I think one of the biggest challenges I find as a franchisor is knowing that you're responsible for your franchisee and their profitability and I think it's a huge responsibility. These people are coming to your business and your brand and often, they're putting their house on the line to open this business.

"We always do the market research first"

I think, as a franchisor, having the responsibility of making this business model work. You have to think about their family and the children that may have to move out of their homes.

> "Our franchisees are our business partners too"

It's a good challenge to have because as a franchisor it keeps you honest in your franchisee selection. It's hard to say "No" to growth from my perspective or from any business perspective. Saying "No" to that extra revenue and brand awareness, I think that's a challenge.

Early on, when people were knocking on our doors saying, "Hey, I really want to buy a franchise," we probably weren't as selective as we are now. However, we've been lucky. All of our franchisees, except one, have been very successful. The one that wasn't successful was removed from the system and we paid them out for their store. It was a good situation in the end.

**So what is the most important thing that you have learned about successful franchising?**

Definitely collaboration. Working collectively and collaboratively with our franchisees. The most important thing I've learned is that our franchisees are our business partners too. We make sure that they're happy and they're supported in the right way. We are not going to go out and do their job for them but we have exceptional relationships with them.

**In your opinion, what are the most common mistakes new franchisors or franchisees make?**

Definitely choosing the wrong people. Not understanding that the relationship is a two-way street. As I said before, that it is a business partnership. It's not necessarily the franchisor constantly preaching to the franchisee. Understanding that franchisees are entrepreneurs as well. That's probably the most common mistake that new franchisors make.

"Both have an obligation to the brand to train themselves"

So from a franchisor's perspective, not training their franchisees, not supporting their franchisees in the right way. Not providing them with a clear plan to their business success. Not providing franchisees with the right training documentation and support mechanisms. Not providing them with the right local area marketing plans and initiatives.

I think mistakes that new franchisees can make is thinking that the franchisor is going to run their business for them. Franchisees could potentially look to the franchisor for blame when things aren't going right in their business, rather than looking at themselves and how they're contributing to the brand or maybe behaving in that area.

Both franchisees and franchisors both have an obligation to the brand to train themselves to the best of their ability within their roles and positions.

"Successful franchisors need to stay ahead of the game"

**What do you believe are the essential qualities and/or attributes of a successful franchisor or franchise system?**

A successful franchisor needs to have a business model that they know is profitable and current. I think franchisors always need to be testing and measuring the franchise system. Is it still relevant to the consumer? Are services or products still priced at the same price? Successful franchisors need to stay ahead of the game and technology in their industry and the technologies that it takes to run that industry as well.

Franchisors need to be leading their franchisees with the latest training, the latest local area marketing and the latest operational support.

> "You need to take a chance."

**What advice would you give someone who is thinking about investing in a franchise?**

I would say lots of research. So, if you've chosen one particular franchise, maybe look at several different franchises in that sector and compare them. I'd say don't listen to the sales person, listen to the franchisees of that system and take on board what they have to say. Are they happy? Are they profitable? Does the franchise system deliver what it's promising to the franchisees? Any sales person from a franchise, whether it's me or another franchisor or a sales person, is only ever going to tell you the great things about the brand.

Every brand and every business has its great points and its downside. That's business, that's life.

**From your perspective, what stops people from being successful?**

Themselves. It's an easy answer, isn't it? Not wanting to take that risk and "risk" sounds like a terrible word, but it's not. It's just going out and weighing up opportunities.

It's their insecurities. There are times in life when you just need to take a leap. You need to take a chance.

**What do you believe are the essential qualities or personal attributes of a successful person?**

It's just drive, focus, a willingness to learn and educate themselves. I believe being positive. Always looking for the positive in a situation or the solution to a situation.

"You need to get out there. You need to do it."

**What do you think holds people back from achieving their goals?**

Fear of failure. Is that financial failure? Is that being embarrassed because things didn't work out? I also think what holds a lot of people back from achieving their goals is having no goals in the first place.

**How would you describe your management style?**

Firm, fair and fun.

I love hearing from other people. I love hearing their feedback, even if it's negative.

I'm always very happy and comfortable to make a decision and to be authoritative when needed.

**What are your secrets to being a successful businesswoman?**

This is one of my secrets; this is what I seriously have to do. At times, I just have to give myself a mantra and just say, "You're Francesca Webster. You're the CEO of this company. You need to get out there. You need to do it. Pull yourself together." I literally have to self-coach myself sometimes, but only a very few times.

For instance, recently, I danced at Brisbane City Hall for a charity event and I danced a disco samba in front of 500 people. I've never danced before in my life. I did about 20 dance lessons and I dressed up as a Brazilian showgirl. I'm 42 years old!

Maybe you have to go and speak publicly somewhere or maybe you have got to do something that's a little bit different or out of your comfort zone. You just have to do it!

But seriously, I just love what I do. I feel very comfortable with what I do and making decisions. I love my brand. I love the people that I work for. I love our franchisees. I love that our franchisees are entrepreneurial and challenging at times. It fits me like a glove and I'm lucky that I've found that in my life.

**How do you stay focused and on track daily and long-term, especially when things are getting a bit tough?**
You've just got to have a plan. We have a strategic plan that's probably the size of a massive textbook but we've actually broken that down to a very simple two or three-page business plan. So we're on track and everything runs to plan.

I attend a lot of events. People invite me along to things and I attend and every time I go along, I learn something or something else is brought to mind.

I also have a mentor. I've had mentors in the past who were different people within my life.

I'm very fortunate in that my mentor, he's only been mentoring me now for a few months, is Tom Potter, the founder of Eagle Boys. He's been popping in and 'kicking my ass for me' as I would call it. That's how I stay focused. By educating myself, by learning new industry trends, by having a plan and trying at all costs to stick to that plan.

**Who would you say has inspired you in the past?**
Definitely Sheryl Sandberg. I just get inspired by so many people. I really do. I love hearing people speak. I recently heard Alisa Camplin

speak and I heard the lady who got burned running in the marathon, Turia Pitt. Completely inspirational.

"There are inspirational people everywhere in our lives."

I think there are inspirational people every*where in our lives.* They are people who do things, stay focused and achieve their goals and objectives, whether those goals and objectives are to get married and have a family, open their own business or run a marathon. I think there's inspiration everywhere.

**As a successful businesswoman, what do you hope to inspire in others?**

The fact that I don't have tertiary education; you don't need tertiary education to go out and open your own business, even though it's probably a great thing to have.

Set yourself some goals, stick to those goals and achieve whatever you want. Follow your dreams. Throw it out there, give it a go, whatever it is that you're looking to do in life.

I would like to inspire our team members and our franchisees to be the best that they can be for the brand.

I'd like to think that I consistently inspire positive change in the business.

"Follow your dreams."

**What does success mean to you? How does one achieve it or have more of it?**

I think I'm pretty driven and can be easily satisfied when we do achieve. Success, to me, means completing the tasks and goals that I've set for myself. Learning from other people and having external people, for want of a better word, 'kick my ass' when I don't achieve what I've said I'm going to.

> "Always make sure that there's a buyer there."

**What is the most important piece of advice anyone has ever given you?**

Gosh, probably loads. A female friend of mine, she's super successful, owns this massive international electronics business and she has this philosophy that she will never make an electronics product unless she knows that she can sell it. She makes hundreds of thousands of these things. She always makes sure that there's a buyer there.

If you're planning on doing something, always make sure that there's a buyer there. As we've expanded Brazilian Beauty, that's been a great piece of advice for me because when we're looking at bringing in another treatment category or we've got salespeople coming in trying to sell us things, we never make that decision. We always do the research to see if we can actually sell it.

Another good piece of advice that a really good friend of mine always says to me is, "Wear the dress. Don't let the dress wear you." It's kind of "Own it!"

> "Wear the dress. Don't let the dress wear you."

**What drives you to continue and to grow?**

Clearly, I just love what I do. I just want to hit that goal. I want to hit that goal of 50 franchisees. It's about the challenge. It's about the challenge more than it is the money.

I want my children to be well cared for and well looked after which, I think, is any parent's instinct and drive.

> "Do it. Do it now."

Also, at some stage in the future, I would like to totally free up my time and have the ability to apply my skill set to a charitable cause.

**Is there a significant quote or saying which you live your life by?**

I've got this Will Smith quote that I absolutely love.

It says, "You might be smarter than me. You might be better looking than me. You might have more money than me but get on a treadmill with me and one of two things will happen. You will get off or I will die. It's that simple."

That's kind of how I feel. I suppose I'm quite competitive.

I have another one, which is, "Do it. Do it now." You know how people say, "I'll do that in a minute" or "I'll do that in five minutes?" I'm like, "Do it, do it now."

**What are some of your future plans or goals for the next 5 to 10 years?**

Over the next five years we would be clearly hitting the 50 stores.

I will take the ASI product internationally. I'm going over to Vegas in July to start that process. I will look for US investment as well as distribution.

Once I hit that goal of 50, Brazilian Beauty will have a new CEO and I will sit on the board.

**What is your greatest passion in life?**
Definitely my family. I think that is a definite. Having fun with my friends and family in whatever form that takes. I just love my family, being around them, doing things with them, providing for them and spoiling them.

I also own, with my partner, a cattle and sheep property; a farm. So I love that place but I am competitive and I love winning as well.

**How do you want to be remembered?**
Actually, that's a really good question. I love Brazilian Beauty but I do not want Brazilian Beauty to be my only business legacy so I'd just like to be remembered as somebody that was intelligent, fun and made things happen.

*There are times in life when you just need to take a leap. You need to take a chance.*

# CHAPTER 9

## ROSE VIS

VIP Home Services

# CHAPTER 9

## **ROSE VIS -**
VIP Home Services

*It is important to know what motivates people to get the best out of them and it is not always money.*

Before the influences and benefits of technology, Rose Vis was building a well-respected business and franchise, VIP Home Services, that has grown, developed and changed with the ever changing world.

VIP Home Services has over 100 franchisees in Australia and New Zealand, employing thousands of people across the brand.

Rose has and continues to massively contribute to the franchising industry. She has served on the South Australian committee of the Franchise Council of Australia for over ten years. She is the current President of the South Australian FCA chapter and sits on the national board of the Franchise Council of Australia.

Rose was the proud recipient of the FCA Franchise Woman of the Year in 2005 for South Australia and in 2012 she was recognised by the Franchise Council of Australia for her contribution to franchising.

Rose enjoys passing her knowledge on to others especially when she helps people become a success in their own right and then they can go on to share that knowledge with others.

During my interview with Rose it was evident that she had faced every challenge that comes with business and franchising and has held her integrity and her values in high regard as a pioneer in the franchising industry. Thank you, Rose.

**Tell us a little bit about yourself and your company**

I was born in India in a place called Ranchi. My dad was a doctor and he worked in the Catholic mission hospitals. My early education was provided by my mum because there weren't a lot of alternatives in the places that my dad chose live.

We left India because of political tensions that were happening and we moved to the UK. My formal schooling started in England at around the age of seven or eight. After two years, we moved to Guyana, which is in South America.

We had seven years in Guyana then we went back to the UK. At age 15, we came to Australia. That was in 1966. My dad bought a practice in Peterborough, four hours north of Adelaide, which is a railway town of approximately a couple of thousand people. I went to the local high school and after I graduated (we didn't go past year 11 in Peterborough) I did voluntary work at the high school to get some experience so that I could get a reference.

When we went to Adelaide in 1969, I got a job as a shorthand typist in an insurance company. I was there for seven years, during which time I met my husband and who is now my business partner in V.I.P. He was in fact the entrepreneur, I would say, in my life and business.

In 1972 we were engaged to be married. We bought a small lawn mowing round which my husband operated on the weekends for extra money. This developed and he then bought and sold various rounds. He discovered that on the weekend he was earning more than in his full-time job. He stopped lawn mowing because lawn mowing wasn't a 'proper' job in those days and went into a sales career. We engaged several contractors to look after the work while he did his sales job. My two brothers, for example, ran the lawn mowing rounds while they were studying at university.

We became involved with a car business but unfortunately the partnership didn't go well. After some time we basically went back to lawn mowing. We grew to about ten casual contractors and continued to grow. We started to develop knowledge about marketing areas and started to organise 'group buying.' We set up arrangements with equipment, uniforms, insurance and so on and then we started to buy and sell rounds again.

I was largely involved with customer relations, looking after the phones, contractors, customers and invoicing. While all that was happening, we started a family.

In 1979, the company was incorporated and we sold our first official franchise. Up until we had approximately 25 franchises, we would have meetings at home and it was all very friendly and close. We used to exchange ideas, have pizza and a few beers.

After 25, we started to set up area managers. For every 10 to 20 franchisees, we would have an area manager who trained and mentored the new franchisees. We engaged a lawyer and an accountant who basically grew with us and specialised in franchising and they have been pivotal in our development.

At that time, systems were very different and there were no such things as answering machines. We didn't have agreements, templates, manuals or guides to tell us what to do and how to do it. I used to start my calls at 6:00am in the morning and would go to about 10:00pm at night. It was all very, very personal. I did enjoy that side of it but we drew minimal wages.

We developed a fairly comprehensive computer system for ourselves and for our franchisees, maintaining the customers, the performances, accounts, walkthrough areas, territories and so on.

We also sought out people who had some knowledge in all types of areas at that time. We were naive about a lot of things, especially with our systems but we learnt by our mistakes.

> "Our focus is sales, education and support."

In 1987, we expanded interstate and in 1991 we granted master franchises in each of the states. I remained in Adelaide and I had a couple of admin girls by that time and a manager. As it developed, I also did most of the work for interstate which meant whatever needed to be done with accounts, customer information and so on.

Up to this point, we were only doing lawn mowing. In 1994, we extended the range of services. We went quite broad. It included ironing, mobile car washing, dog washing, mobile mechanics, pool cleaning and carpet cleaning. After some time, we essentially focused on lawn mowing, gardening and cleaning of windows and carpets.

We also expanded to New Zealand and now have approximately 1,100 franchises. I just received notice that we have another 30-year franchisee, which we always recognise with a token, for example a watch. We also recognise 20 year franchisees too.

We have support managers and we believe that is key to our development. We engage consultants and advisers for other matters, such as legal advice and writing documentation.

Our focus is sales, education and support. Our support team meets with franchisees regularly. A lot of focus is being put into our online presence for better communication and online education. Each franchisee can have their own web page which can be customised to promote their expertise with photographs and testimonials.

> "We had a proven system"

Our marketing team assists with local area marketing, so we encourage them to promote themselves in the local community, sports clubs, community groups, etc.

**What do you think are some of the factors that contributed to your company's exciting growth?**

Timing, because V.I.P were the first home service organisation to franchise in Australia and we were the only system around at that time. Other lawn mowing operators and contractors were fairly unprofessionally presented. There was no signage, no uniform or system and we developed a lot of the things that we now realise was a franchise. We designed a very professional trailer, not only for the equipment but to be a billboard to advertise the brand.

We maximised our marketing impact as an individual lawn contractor did not have the funds to advertise on TV or have a full-colour page in the Yellow Pages. Buying as a group was much more effective.

We had a proven system because we ran the business for seven years before we franchised. We engaged professional legal, financial and marketing advice right from the onset.

**What are some of the most exciting changes you've experienced?"**

From a manual system, books and pens, to fully-computerised systems. Phone call communication is another big one. Now we have our own support centre. We allocate work to franchisees, take their calls and provide a help line. We have SMS messaging, mobile phones, handheld merchant facilities and that sort of thing. Gone are the days of the fax machine and photocopiers.

"When you're starting you have to be patient."

We put a lot of emphasis on monthly meetings. Now, there are webinars, online courses and so on. I would say that a lot of the change is largely in technology.

**What do you believe is your biggest sacrifice in getting the business off the ground?**

When you're starting you have to be patient. You have to put yourself last. We invested everything back into the business and we ended up selling our home to finance the business. Initially we purchased trailers for the business so we could hire out the trailers to franchisees. Working from home for many years, it meant 24/7, if necessary.

My family had to grow up very quickly and I missed out on things like sports days.

**If there was one key area in management you would do differently, what would it be?**

There are probably quite a few things that we'd probably do differently. I think we'd be more strategic in how we expanded, for example, interstate, perhaps more slowly and with more of a reason, rather than saying, "Oh, one of the franchisees is going to Perth. We'll go to Perth!" We'd probably be a bit more strategic and put a bit more research into areas. At the time we didn't have the greatest knowledge or expertise in this area of business.

"It inspires me to feel that we are a respected franchisor."

We would look at the selection processes differently. I would be bit less emotionally involved when appointing franchisees or master franchisees.

**What would you say have been the highlights for your business?**

I think the biggest one is the fact that we have lasted in the industry for over 36 years as a franchise company and it inspires me to feel that we are a respected franchisor. That the brand is recognised and respected and when you talk to a perfect stranger, they recognise it and you think, "My God, that's my company" and being proud of myself.

Hearing the franchisees' stories of their success and watching personal and financial development. Being proud of the staff who have what we call, "green blood."

"Learn from people who are smarter than you are."

**What tips would you give to other businesswomen who are getting into business?**

To not give up! Not to expect things to happen too quickly. Learn from people who are smarter than you are. Do more networking. In the last five to ten years I have networked more than I ever did before.

You have to like what you do. After all this time, I still really like what I do. I miss some things like not being involved in the day-to-day running of the business. I do miss that contact at times.

There are so many ways you can learn. You can talk to people. You can search it online. I suggest get as much information as you can.

**When did you first discover that you had entrepreneurial talent?**

I've always been a little uncomfortable with that title. I have never credited myself with being the entrepreneur in the business as I always thought Bill was the entrepreneur. However, I believe I'm very good at recognising what is good for the business. I think I'm a better judge of character and I can get the best out of people without having to throw my weight around or thump my fists.

**What was your approach to marketing and how did you get the name of the business into the marketplace?**

Originally, the prime area was the Yellow Pages and we had a White Pages listing in bold. We were very prominent. We don't utilise Yellow Pages any more but we used the local paper and also pamphlets. Our budget has been redirected into television and online.

**What are your tips for effectively branding the business?**

The first thing was the trailers for our lawn mowing contractors. As I said, each unit is like a billboard.

We did lots of sponsorships wherever there was an opportunity to get the name out, whether it was for the sporting venue or a local club. If a franchisee wants to sponsor their local bowls, we're all for it.

We prioritise local area marketing at every opportunity. Everything that we can do that gets the brand out there, we will do. Being on the committee of the Franchise Council of Australia is a way of getting our brand out there as well.

**When did you know that it was time to think about franchising the brand?**

It was accidental because of the way that we had originally set it up. We aligned ourselves to being a cooperative, so we were a co-op that was buying blades for mowers or spark plugs or invoice books in bulk to get the better price for the members because that's what our job was, I thought.

Then businesses were coming to Australia, particularly from America, like McDonald's that was tagged as a franchise. All of a sudden, it was like, "That's what we do. We're a franchise." That was in 1979.

**How did you promote and sell those first new franchises?**

Traditional ways of business partnerships. Business partnerships and franchise magazines, that was primarily it. We also had a lot of word of mouth. We had a franchisee and he brought in one of his nephews and that nephew brought in his brother, so word of mouth was good.

**How do you think the branding has evolved from start up to now?**

The brand has been fairly traditional in how we have evolved.

We'd like it to be as recognisable as a Nike tick. The floral shape in our logo represents the petal of a flower, the swirl of a mop, blades of a lawn mower and a whirlwind of opportunity. It would be great if consumers could recognise it without having the V.I.P. text. We still have a way to go when you say, "What is V.I.P. Home Services?" It's not immediately recognisable in every place. It's more recognisable in Adelaide because we started there. Sometimes you have to explain a little more about what V.I.P. Home Services actually is.

> "It fast-tracked the development in many ways."

**What has been one of the biggest challenges you've had to face in the franchise business and how did you overcome it?**

Developing some of the technological advances, for example, one of the challenges that we had originally was, in fact, going to pager because we were wondering why we were losing work. In Melbourne particularly, they were saying, "Well, I've been going to jobs and someone else has gotten ahead of me." Our competitor had pagers and they were on it and we were slower at accepting the paging systems. That's when we said, "That's it! We have got to go to pagers."

Another challenge is the fact that we went into master franchising. It was great for our development. It fast-tracked the development in many ways. Challenge-wise, we had very determined, strong-minded people with strong opinions in their character. That presented some challenges, particularly if things didn't happen the way the individual wanted it to.

For example: We had national splits of contribution. If there was a national campaign, Tasmania contributed X percentage whereas Melbourne contributed a larger percentage. We have had some challenges with master franchisees and the acceptance of this structure and have now bought back most of our territories.

New Zealand and Tasmania still have a master franchise in place and we've got some small service masters in Queensland, Albury and Wodonga.

"You have to make sure that there is an ongoing demand."

**What is the most important thing you've learned about successful franchising?**

Not everything can be put into a franchise model. You have to make sure that there is an ongoing demand. You can't get your lawn cut on the internet, for example, and you can't get your house cleaned on the internet. Luckily, you can source someone to do it for you.

I think the right person is always important because just getting a franchise fee from someone is not going to be a good fit for the long term.

**What are the most common mistakes new franchisors and franchisees make?**

I think you should trial it first. As I said, we operated for seven years before franchising.

Underestimating the cost of establishing a franchise. Not establishing sound foundations, not making sure that their documentation and their manual support systems are strong.

Over-promising and definitely under-delivering.

"The franchisee may have unreasonably high expectations of a franchisor."

The franchisee may have unreasonably high expectations of a franchisor. They might underestimate the hard work that is involved, underestimating the time needed to establish the business.

Underestimating the capital investment and not asking enough questions, not asking for help soon enough and lack of family support is huge. Overspending or not budgeting and the number of people who don't allow for their GST is a problem.

One of the things which comes with not asking enough questions is that they might not fully understand the franchise relationship and their obligations, even though they've read it and been told it.

**What do you believe are the essential qualities and attributes of the successful franchisor?**

An established brand and a proven system and the model. Our communication to the franchisees and staff is more and more transparent. "This is what happened. This is why we do it. This is how much we're getting."

You have to have good training in the staff, I think that's hugely important. They need ongoing support.

Image, good marketing, budget, strategies and their advertising. The territory is important. Opportunities for advancement of any kind.

**What advice you would give someone who is thinking about investing in a franchise?**

The number one thing would be to research and do your due diligence. Ask questions. People do their research online a lot more and come to us already knowing about the industry and about us. We encourage them to talk to existing franchisees and to go out for a day or couple of days in the field.

"It is important to know what motivates people to get the best out of them"

**What stops people from being successful?**

Lack of confidence and belief in your product or system. Lack of interest or empathy with your franchisees and those you work with. It is important to know what motivates people to get the best out of them and it is not always money. I don't like people who are disrespectful towards their franchisees and people they work with. I say "work with," not "work for." I feel more comfortable because a lot of our systems have evolved from the observations and recommendations of franchisees.

You've got to persevere and basically ride with the punches and have a "never give up" type of attitude.

**What are the essential qualities or personal attributes of a successful person?**

Good communication skills, strategic thinking, being a good listener, knowing what people want or need and being perceptive. You need to be a bit of an entrepreneur and imagination and determination is important as is perseverance. You need to be patient and empathetic. The thing that gets forgotten is common sense. You need to have some common sense, logical thinking and problem solving skills.

"Acknowledge your mistakes and learn from them."

Acknowledge achievements that people make. Also acknowledge your mistakes and learn from them. You've got to be positive and accept that you have to make personal sacrifices and as I said once before, genuinely love what you do and like people because you're in a people business.

"Have passionate people that you work with."

**What do you think holds people back from achieving their goals?**

I'll summarise it by saying, not having all of the above. Not having all of those attributes.

**How would you describe your management style?**

I like to think that I have led by example as much as possible, partly because I've had to but there was no one else around to do it. I had my part in the business and Bill had his part.

I like to think I'm a fair and good communicator. I like to have fair dealings with staff, franchisees and associates. I certainly endeavour to create a great working environment.

**What are your secrets to being a successful businesswoman?**

Surround yourself with people who are smarter than yourself

Have passionate people that you work with. You must have a passion for what you do and enjoy sharing that with other people. Passion is very infectious. I love going to the conferences for that reason. You have your yearly major injection. You need to listen to other successful people and learn from them and never give up!

**How did you stay focused and on track especially when times got tough?**

I don't allow myself to entertain the negative thoughts. Sometimes I may say, "I don't think this will work," for example: if something's going wrong, if we need to resolve something, I like to think "Okay, it will work and we make it happen."

> "I don't allow myself to entertain the negative thoughts."

No matter how bad things are, tomorrow's another day and tomorrow's always better.

By prioritising what's got to be done. As they say, "You can only eat an elephant one bite at a time," so from that point of view you have to prioritise and work through your list.

**Who would you say has inspired you in the past?**

There have been lots and lots of people and there still are and there always will be. Somebody that did impress me and still does after hearing her at one of the franchise conferences was Dr. Fiona Wood. She's the head of the Royal Perth Hospital Burns Unit. I've also read about her and I was very inspired by her because she has achieved so much in her career academically and she helps others. She's always conducting research and advanced treatments for burns victims. She's also a mother of six and a grandmother. I think that it's amazing that you can do whatever you want to. She has six kids and I felt quite insignificant, to be quite honest. I think she's just an amazing person.

**As a top successful businesswoman, what do you hope to inspire in others?**

To believe in themselves. I was a very insecure and very shy person, then I was pushed way out of my comfort zone. Many, many times I thought, "I can't do this. I just can't do this." But I did! I think you need to believe in yourself, you have to, particularly when you're pushed out of your comfort zone.

> "You need to take emotion out of it."

**What does success mean to you and how do you achieve it?**
I'm really proud of the business that I've helped to build and a business that's provided a good living for many families, thousands in fact!

I get to pass on knowledge to other people, the franchisees and some of the staff that become successful in their own right.

Franchisees who we have trained and who shine in particular areas and are now training others to do what they're doing. That is a success to know that you've contributed to something that's good and great.

**What is the most important piece of advice anyone has ever given you?**
A person said to me, "To make a good decision, a balanced decision, first, you need to take emotion out of it." I've learnt over the years what she meant by that. I was involved in a lot of the mediations and reconciliations with franchisees and masters. When you've been in a situation where you've been to their house or you've had dinner and then you have to make a difficult decision, you do have to take the emotion out of it.

Another one that I have heard over and over again is, "The definition of insanity - doing the same thing over and over again and expecting a different result."

**What drives you to keep going and still be a part of this growing business?**
I care about it. I do still enjoy it and I'm really enjoying the fact that

things can always be better. We can always learn and I'm enjoying watching that happen. It's a bit more youthful, it's perhaps a younger world now and it's exciting to watch.

If we keep improving and give people the freedom to exercise their expertise, things will get even better. The system will be one that is a franchise of choice, rather than us having to market heavily. I'd like to see that happen.

### Is there a significant quote or saying that you live your life by?

Audrey Hepburn, one of her quotes is, "I believe in pink. I believe that laughing is the best calorie counter. I believe in kissing, kissing a lot. I believe in being strong when everything seems to be going wrong. I believe that happy girls are the prettiest girls. I believe that tomorrow is another day and I believe in miracles."

### What are some of your future plans and goals?

I'm no longer in the day-to-day running of the business but I'm involved with the Franchise Council of Australia. I'm the President of the South Australian chapter. I enjoy these roles and having that interaction.

I'm trying to travel somewhere at least once a year. I'm spending more time with my family. Because of the business, with my own kids I missed some of their childhood and I feel a little bit guilty about this so I'm looking forward to sharing that more with my grandchildren.

I would like to watch V.I.P. continue to develop. I've always aspired to — it doesn't sound much but I have always wanted V.I.P. to achieve 4% of the market share. So that'd be really nice.

**What is your greatest passion in life?**

Hearing people say that joining V.I.P. was the best decision they'd ever made. I like hearing about people who are passionate about what they do; that makes me feel the same way.

**How do you want to be remembered?**

I would like to be remembered as an ordinary person, who has made a significant contribution to the franchise industry and as one of the pioneers of Australian franchising. Someone who faced challenges. Someone who helped create an enduring brand that has provided thousands of people with an opportunity and lifestyle beyond their expectations.

*We had a proven system because we ran the business for seven years before we franchised.*

# ABOUT THE AUTHOR

## Sharon Jurd

**Entrepreneur, Author, Speaker, Business Mentor and Success Coach**

Sharon is a highly respected International best-selling Author as well as a seasoned Business Executive, Entrepreneur, Growth Strategist and Success Coach.

She is passionate about helping people grow their business faster than the competition by giving those business owners financial freedom, and the choice to live the life they deserve.

Sharon is qualified and recognised as a leading business coach, licenced business agent, licenced real estate agent, licenced auctioneer, licenced stock and station agent and she holds a diploma in business and franchising.

Sharon's passion for peak performance and creating success started just 6 months after she opened her first real estate office as a Century 21 franchisee, she obtained a 72% market share despite having six major well established competitors. Within the year Sharon had opened her second office and quickly became a major player in that market place too – as the youngest single female director within the organization.

After dominating in this area Sharon went looking for a new challenge and sold her successful awarding winning real estate offices.

Sharon is the director of her own franchise network "HydroKleen Australia" and grew it massively in just 2 short years making it the leader in its field.

Her professional achievements have been recognized by her winning over 17 industry and business awards such as Franchise Business of the Year, People's Choice Award, Chamber of Commerce

Business of the Year, Gold Coast Business Excellence Award - Emerging Business and Merit Award for Franchise Women of the Year NT/QLD just to name a few.

For more than 20 years Sharon has worked, travelled, consulted and taught internationally, speaking to and motivating thousands of people in Australia, New Zealand, England, France, Italy, United Arab

Emirates, USA, and Canada on how to create wealth and financial success.

Sharon's achievement and motivational programs plus articles published in newspapers and magazines nationally and internationally, have made her a sought-after speaker and consultant on the international stage.

She is the International author of the book "How To Grow Your Business Faster Than Your Competitor – *The Secrets to Freedom and Success in 5 easy steps*"

Sharon is a member of many professional bodies and associations including Franchise Council of Australia and Women in Franchising.

She lives in Queensland, Australia with her partner John.

# RESOURCE CENTRE

# RESOURCE CENTRE

## Sharon Jurd Events

Sharon Jurd Events offers a unique experience in business growth, bringing like-minded people together to learn, explore and discover their full potential through seminars, motivational materials, webinars, books and consultations on a range of business subjects.

You'll be shown how to identify exactly what to do to maximise your businesses productivity and profits. You'll also receive specific coaching to help you apply the most important strategies to achieve better profits for far less effort.

Sharon Jurd Events seminars have an impressive format unlike any other you have attended including international guest speakers who are successful in their own right, giving you unprecedented insights into their successes and businesses secrets.

You will also have the opportunity to have quality one-on-one time with the presenters who all have a natural 'giving' attitude to help you grow your business fast.

Sharon Jurd Events provides a range of business educational materials including the international best selling book, *How to Grow Your Business Faster than your Competitors*, and inspirational support material all available through the Sharon Jurd Events website.

With over 20 years experience in growing and building successful national businesses, Sharon Jurd Events delivers seminars, business coaching and mentoring in a an impressive and informative format to show you a proven formula to reach financial freedom and success.

If you're serious about growing your business to its fullest potential, Sharon Jurd Events reaches out to 'Impress the Mind and Move the Feelings'.

**Sharon Jurd Events**
Sharon Jurd
CEO
PO Box 409
Labrador QLD 4215
Australia
0429 686 586
sharonjurd@sharonjurdevents.com.au
www.sharonjurdevents.com.au

## HydroKleen Australia

HydroKleen Australia is a master franchisor that has developed the most comprehensive method for cleaning split system air conditioning units, eliminating a range of contaminants that are commonly found, significantly improving the quality of the air, and reducing power consumption.

HydroKleen was founded in 2009 after extensive research found a need for speeding up the process of servicing and cleaning split system air conditioners, especially given that nearly every household has one or more air conditioner of some sort, and there was no industry standard for the servicing and cleaning of air conditioners.

The HydroKleen system can completely wet wash and sanitise an air conditioner with a no splash, no mess result, and allows for ease of use in people's homes with the facility to carry out a pressure wash without damaging property, a major point of difference within the air conditioning industry.

HydroKleen Australia established its national head office on the Gold Coast in 2010 due to its accessibility and strategic position to the north and south of Australia. Since then the company has grown to 19 franchises Australia wide (as of June 2013) employing over 50 people with many more territories in each state currently under application.

HydroKleen franchisees are primarily air conditioning companies who understand a need to add an additional profit centre to their already existing business.

The HydroKleen model is based around an unlicensed technician as a 'man in the van' application and is proving to be overwhelmingly successful for this market.

**HydroKleen Australia**
John Sanders & Sharon Jurd
Directors
6/12 Tonga Place
Parkwood QLD 4214
Australia
07 557 449 08
service@hydrokleen.com.au
www.hydrokleen.com.au

## Arrow Insurance

Arrow was established in 1999 to provide Insurance and Financial Advice.

The Directors are Steve and Janet Culpitt. Steve has over 30 years experience in the field of financial planning, advice and service. Janet's history is in human resources, staff training, compliance, process and administration.

Steve is a qualified and well respected Financial Adviser and Risk Insurance Specialist in his Industry. He is professionally qualified, compliant with RG146. His qualifications include: Diploma of Financial Planning (DFP) 1, 2, 3, 4 & 5, Margin Lending and SMSF.
Janet's role is Administration Manager and the "Rain Maker" for their business, having proved her expertise and natural ability to meet new contacts and develop relationships that result in both new business and continued growth for all parties.

Combine these attributes and you see why we they are specialists in this area and they are dedicated to providing the appropriate solutions for both businesses and individuals.

Arrow's focus is on assisting clients to protect their lifestyles and to grow wealth. They do this by identifying clients ever changing financial goals and objectives, and then offering tailored, strategic solutions. Customer Service and getting to know their clients and forming long lasting relationships are their priority.

Planning is making smart decisions about money and achieving financial goals.

Arrow's wealth coaching helps you create a clear picture of where you are now, where you want to be and then implement strategies and actions to get there, whilst reviewing regularly to make sure you stay on track.

**Arrow Insurance**
Steve & Janet Culpitt
Directors
PO Box 652
Mudgeeraba QLD 4213
Australia
07 55303 500
info@arrowinsurance.com.a
www.arrowinsurance.com.au

## Bell Partners

Bell Partners has built its reputation as one of Australia's premier boutique accounting & financial advisory firms on the basis of delivering and exceeding our clients expectations. The business model has evolved since its inception in the 1960's by founding principal Donald Bell. A generational change in the late 1990's led to Anthony Bell acquiring the business from his father, with it now in a position of approximately 100 staff across offices in each of the major capital cities, specialising in business consulting, tax advisory, assurance, wealth creation and finance.

We are proud of our business and how we have helped our clients achieve their goals over many years but it is constantly in the forefront of our minds that we cannot rest on our laurels and must continue to innovate. We are proud to act for many successful small business entrepreneurs, up-and-coming talents as well as established home grown businesses. Many of our clients have started with us needing simple individual tax returns and then progressed with our help to operating highly successful businesses in their own right. Our job is to help you get there.

We believe we have the best people working for us in an environment that rewards initiative and strives for success. It is an attitude that keeps us at the leading edge of accounting and related financial service providers. We are excited about the future and opportunities for success as we ride out of the Global Financial Crisis, as we forge ahead together, sharing in the continued success of growth and change.

**Bell Partners**

Darren Morris
Managing Director
Level 3, 164 Grey Street
South Brisbane QLD 4101
Australia
1300 235 575 (1300 BELLQLD)
bellqld@bellpartners.com
www.bellpartners.com

www.ingramcontent.com/pod-product-compliance
Ingram Content Group UK Ltd.
Pitfield, Milton Keynes, MK11 3LW, UK
UKHW020143250726
13967UKWH00002B/834

9 781922 118868